Mentor-Lernhilfe
Band 86

ONE, TWO, THREE GO!

Ein Übungsprogramm
für die 5./6. Klasse   Teil 2

Von Rainer Iwen

Illustrationen von Jutta Bauer

Auflage: 5. 4. 3. 2. | Letzte Zahlen
Jahr: 1987 86 85 84 | maßgeblich

© 1983 by mentor-Verlag Dr. Ramdohr KG, München
Druck: Druckhaus Langenscheidt, Berlin
Printed in Germany. ISBN 3-580-64860-8

Vorwort

Dear Friend,

Ich hoffe, daß Du bei der Arbeit mit dem ersten Teil von ONE, TWO, THREE... GO! viel Spaß und vor allem guten Erfolg in der Schule gehabt hast. Auch der zweite Teil will Dir helfen, Deine vielleicht durch Krankheit oder Unaufmerksamkeit entstandenen Lücken zu schließen und Dein Wissen zu festigen.
Wie ist mit dem Buch zu arbeiten?
Du hast zwei Möglichkeiten:
1. Du arbeitest es von vorn bis hinten durch; gleichsam als Wiederholungskurs zusätzlich zum Englischunterricht in Deiner Klasse. Das Buch ist gestuft aufgebaut und führt Dich vom Einfachen zum Schweren.
2. Du suchst Dir den Stoff, der Dir Schwierigkeiten bereitet, aus dem Inhaltsverzeichnis oder aus dem Stichwortregister heraus und erarbeitest diesen Teil.

Beginne aber jedes Kapital immer am Anfang und arbeite es bis zum Ende durch. Auch die Kapitel sind stufenweise aufgebaut, so daß Du durch die Arbeit mit den Aufgaben Hilfen für die Lösung der weiteren Aufgaben erhältst. Lies die Einführung zu den Übungen genau durch, denn nur wer eine Aufgabe genau verstanden hat, kann sie auch mit Erfolg lösen. Unterstreiche die Wörter, die Du in den Texten

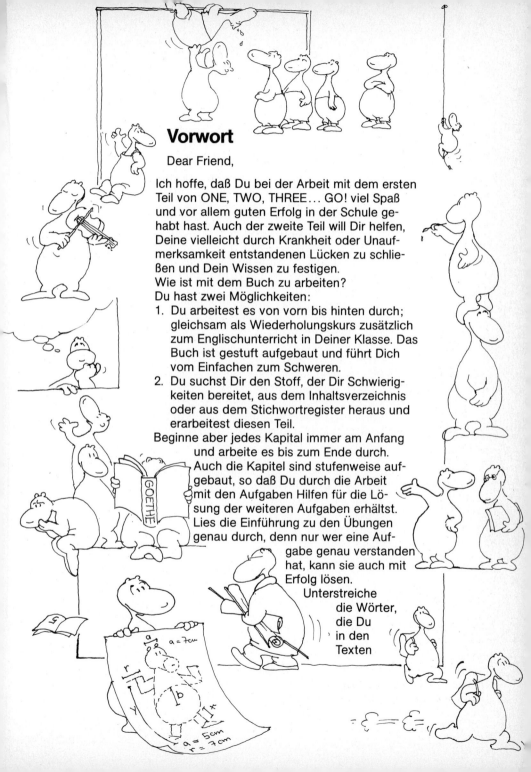

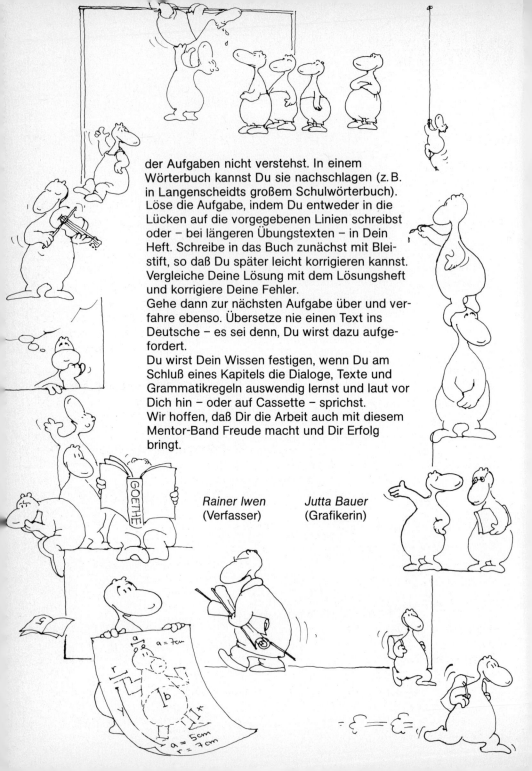

der Aufgaben nicht verstehst. In einem Wörterbuch kannst Du sie nachschlagen (z. B. in Langenscheidts großem Schulwörterbuch). Löse die Aufgabe, indem Du entweder in die Lücken auf die vorgegebenen Linien schreibst oder – bei längeren Übungstexten – in Dein Heft. Schreibe in das Buch zunächst mit Bleistift, so daß Du später leicht korrigieren kannst. Vergleiche Deine Lösung mit dem Lösungsheft und korrigiere Deine Fehler.
Gehe dann zur nächsten Aufgabe über und verfahre ebenso. Übersetze nie einen Text ins Deutsche – es sei denn, Du wirst dazu aufgefordert.
Du wirst Dein Wissen festigen, wenn Du am Schluß eines Kapitels die Dialoge, Texte und Grammatikregeln auswendig lernst und laut vor Dich hin – oder auf Cassette – sprichst.
Wir hoffen, daß Dir die Arbeit auch mit diesem Mentor-Band Freude macht und Dir Erfolg bringt.

Rainer Iwen *Jutta Bauer*
(Verfasser)   (Grafikerin)

INHALT

Vorwort	3
Die Zeichen der internationalen Lautschrift	7

1 Full Verbs – Vollverben   8
Satzstellung, Formen des Verbs – Übersicht über die wichtigsten Verben des Englischen
Übungsziel: Kenntnis der englischen Verben, die im Deutschen leicht verwechselt werden

2 Auxiliaries – Hilfsverben   27
die Formen des Verbs "to be", wie man sich begrüßt, the "there structure", die Formen des Verbs "to have", die Formen des Verbs "to do"
Übungsziel: Aussagesätze, Fragesätze, Verneinung mit den Hilfsverben "to be" – "to have" – "to do"

3 Defective Auxiliaries – Unvollständige Hilfsverben   45
Übersicht über die unvollständigen Hilfsverben und deren Gebrauch; was man sagt, wenn man um Hilfe bittet
Übungsziel: Gebrauch der unvollständigen Hilfsverben in Frage und Verneinung

4 Traffic – Verkehr   59
Verkehrsmittel, Verkehrszeichen
Übungsziel: Anwendung und Gebrauch des unvollständigen Hilfsverbs "must"

5 The Imperative – Die Befehlsform   66
eine Reise um die Welt, Körperteile, Gymnastik
Übungsziel: Anwendung der Befehlsform in verschiedenen Sachgebieten

6 Asking The Way – Telling The Way – Finding The Way   75
Gebäude; nach dem Weg fragen; Wegbeschreibung
Übungsziel: Anwendung der Befehlsform

7 How To Ask Questions – Fragen stellen   82
Einführung in die Umschreibung mit "to do"
Übungsziel: Fragestellung bei Sätzen mit Vollverben, Umschreibung mit "to do"

8 Negation – Verneinung   89
was man mag und was man nicht mag; Berufe
Übungsziel: die Verneinung bei Sätzen mit Vollverben

INHALT

**9 Question Words –
Frageführwörter**   **94**
welche Frageführwörter gibt es?, die Fragestellung mit "who" und "what"; wie man Leute interviewt
Übungsziel: Einführung und Gebrauch der Frageführwörter

10 At The Station   **107**
der Bahnhof, was man am Fahrkartenschalter sagt
Übungsziel: Anwendung der Frageführwörter

11 Question Tags – Kurzfragen   **111**
Einführung in den Gebrauch von Kurzfragen, nicht wahr? – und – oder nicht?
Übungsziel: Anwendung von Frageform und Verneinung mit Hilfsverben und dem Verb "to do"

12 The Tenses – Die Zeitformen des Verbs   **115**
Übersicht über die Zeitstufen
Übungsziel: die Zeitformen des Verbs

**13 The Simple Present Tense –
Die einfache Gegenwart**   **116**
die Formen der einfachen Gegenwart, was man gewöhnlich am Tag und in der Woche tut, Berufe
Übungsziel: die einfache Gegenwart

**14 The Continuous Form –
Die Verlaufsform**   **136**
die Verlaufsform in der Gegenwart, Freizeitaktivitäten, Brief über die Schule
Übungsziel: Übung und Gebrauch der Verlaufsform in der Gegenwart

**15 The Past Tense –
Die einfache Vergangenheit**   **146**
regelmäßige und unregelmäßige Verben; was man am Wochenende tat; das Märchen vom Rotkäppchen
Übungsziel: die Bildung der Vergangenheitsform, Frage, Verneinung, Verlaufsform in der Vergangenheit

**16 The Present Perfect Tense –
Die vollendete Gegenwart**   **163**
Helfen im Haushalt, was man jemals oder niemals getan hat, "signal words" für die vollendete Gegenwart
Übungsziel: Übung und Gebrauch der vollendeten Gegenwart

17 Contractions – Verkürzungen   **174**
Einführung in die verkürzten Formen der Verben
Übungsziel: Kurzformen

Index – Stichwortverzeichnis   **176**

Die Zeichen der Internationalen Lautschrift

1. Allgemeine Zeichen

Die Lautschrift erscheint immer in eckigen Klammern: English [ˈingliʃ].
Vor der betonten Silbe steht ein Betonungszeichen (Akzent) [ˈ].
Die Länge eines Selbstlauts wird durch [ː] bezeichnet.

2. Die englischen Selbstlaute

[ɑː]	park	[pɑːk]	[i]	drink	[driŋk]
[æ]	man	[mæn]	[ɔ]	not	[nɔt]
[ʌ]	come	[kʌm]	[ɔː]	four	[fɔː]
[ə]	a	[ə]	[u]	look	[luk]
[əː]	sir	[səː]			

3. Die englischen Doppelselbstlaute

In allen englischen Doppelselbstlauten wird der erste Bestandteil stärker gesprochen als der zweite, der nur ein leichter Nachklang ist.

[ei]	name	[neim]	[ɛə]	hair	[hɛə]
[ai]	I	[ai]	[uə]	tourist	[ˈtuərist]
[au]	now	[nau]	[ɔi]	boy	[bɔi]
[iə]	here	[hiə]	[əu]	go	[gəu]

4. Die englischen Mitlaute

[l]	late	[leit]	[w]	will	[wil]
	old	[əuld]	[s]	service	[ˈsəːvis]
	full	[ful]	[z]	is	[iz]
[r]	park	[pɑːk]	[ʃ]	shop	[ʃɔp]
	right	[rait]	[ʒ]	just	[dʒʌst]
[ŋ]	long	[lɔŋ]	[θ]	think	[θiŋk]
[v]	very	[ˈveri]	[ð]	the	[ðə]

1 FULL VERBS

Part 1 Word order and verb forms

Satzstellung und die Form des Verbs
Verben sind die Kernstücke des Satzes. Ihre Hauptaufgabe im Satz ist die Bildung des Prädikats, der <u>Satzaussage</u>, weil sie aussagen, was das Subjekt, der <u>Satzgegenstand</u>, tut oder was mit ihm geschieht.

1. **Translation exercise**

Translate the sentences
Sieh Dir diese Sätze an und übersetze sie.

	subject	verb	object
1	my father	drinks	milk
2	Peggy	eats	cake
3	they	play	table tennis
4	cows	eat	grass

1. *Mein Vater trinkt Milch.*

2. *Peggy*

3. _____

4. _____

Answer the questions in English.
Nun beantworte die Fragen auf englisch.

1. Was wird über Vater ausgesagt? *My father drinks milk.*

2. Was wird über Peggy ausgesagt? _____

3. Was wird über sie ausgesagt? _____

4. Was wird über die Kühe ausgesagt? _____

Das Verb verbindet das Subjekt und das Objekt. Es sagt etwas über das Subjekt aus.

2. Forms of the verbs

Verben können Zeiten – **tenses** – bilden und sagen aus, wann, wie lange schon oder wie häufig etwas geschieht.
Hier ist eine Übersicht über die Formen des Verbs, die in diesem Buch behandelt werden.
Die einzelnen Formen kannst Du auf den entsprechenden Seiten üben.

names of the verb forms	examples Beispiele	tenses Zeiten	Seiten
simple present tense forms **-s** form	I they learn English you Mr. X (he) the girl (she) learn|s| English it	Die einfache Gegenwartsform	116 ↓ 129
continuous/ progressive -ing forms am/is/are + verb + -ing	I am learning English you are learning English he/she/it is learning English we are learning English you are learning English they are learning English	Die Verlaufsform in der Gegenwart	136 ↓ 145
past tense forms **-ed** form (regular)	you watch|ed| TV last night	Die Vergangenheit	146 ↓ 161
special forms (irregular)	you |saw| a Mickey Mouse film		
-ing form (past) was/were + verb -ing	he |was| sitt|ing| in the living-room we |were| sitt|ing| in the living-room	Die Verlaufsform in der Vergangenheit	161 ↓ 162

past participle forms have/has + **-ed** form	I have watched TV he has watched TV	Die vollendete Gegenwart (present perfect)	163 ↓ 173
have/has + special form	you have learnt English he has learnt English		163 ↓ 176

Part 2   Full verbs (Vollverben)

1. Wir unterscheiden **full verbs** (Vollverben) und **auxiliaries** (Hilfsverben) (siehe Seite 45).
"Full verbs" können – wie im Deutschen – eine **Tätigkeit** oder einen **Zustand** bezeichnen.

*Hier sind einige Verben, die der Bedeutung nach zusammengehören.
Lerne sie auswendig!*

to eat	= essen	to drink	= trinken
to sleep	= schlafen	to wake up	= aufwachen
to rest	= ruhen	to work	= arbeiten
		to play	= spielen
to live	= leben	to stay	= wohnen
to climb	= klettern	to creep	= kriechen
to ride	= reiten	to drive	= fahren
to pass	= vorbeifahren		
to swim	= schwimmen	to sink	= sinken
to fly	= fliegen		
to hear	= hören	to see	= sehen
to taste	= schmecken	to listen (to)	= zuhören
to clean	= säubern	to polish	= polieren
to wash	= waschen	to wipe	= wischen
to brush	= bürsten		
to build	= bauen	to dig	= graben

to buy	= kaufen	to sell	= verkaufen
to pay	= bezahlen	to steal	= stehlen
to fight	= kämpfen	to shoot	= schießen
to hurt	= verletzen	to kick	= (mit dem Fuß) stoßen schießen (im Fußball)
to hide	= verstecken	to lose	= verlieren
to find	= finden		
to help	= helfen	to follow	= folgen
to meet	= treffen		
to use	= gebrauchen	to wear	= tragen
to exchange	= tauschen		
to know	= wissen	to understand	= verstehen
to remember	= erinnern	to forget	= vergessen
to teach	= lehren	to learn	= lernen
to rain	= regnen	to shine	= scheinen
to think	= denken	to believe	= glauben
to expect	= erwarten	to hope	= hoffen
to go	= gehen	to come	= kommen
to stop	= halten	to wait	= warten
to stand up	= aufstehen	to sit (down)	= sich (hin)setzen
to lie (down)	= sich hinlegen	to fall	= fallen
to get up	= aufstehen		
to point at	= auf etwas zeigen	to look at	= ansehen
		to show	= zeigen
to throw	= werfen	to catch	= fangen
to drop	= fallen lassen	to pick up	= aufsammeln
to break	= brechen	to cut	= schneiden
to tear	= reißen	to burn	= brennen
to give	= geben	to send	= senden
to lend	= (ver)leihen	to get	= bekommen
to fetch	= holen	to bring	= (mit-, her)bringen
to carry	= tragen	to take	= hinbringen
to keep	= behalten	to give back	= zurückgeben

to read	= lesen	to write	= schreiben
to draw	= zeichnen		
to say	= sagen	to speak	= sprechen
to ask	= fragen	to tell	= erzählen
to call	= rufen	to answer	= antworten
		to begin	= beginnen
to start	= anfangen	to go on	= weitermachen
to finish	= beenden	to stop	= anhalten

2. Funny pictures

Have a look at the pictures and write the verbs.
Sieh Dir jetzt die Bilder an und schreibe die Tätigkeitswörter darunter.
Achtung! Schau nicht auf den Seiten 10–12 nach.

to w . k . . p

to p . . y

to w . . k

to r . s .

to r . . em . . .

to p . l . s .

to . . . ch

to . ai .

to b . . sh

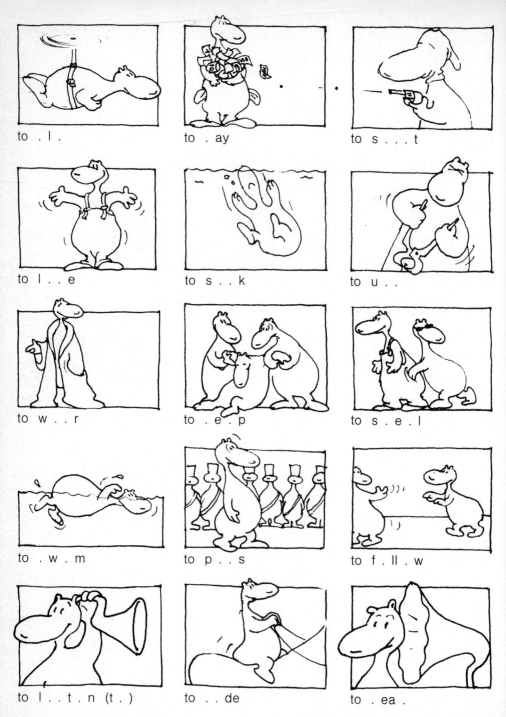

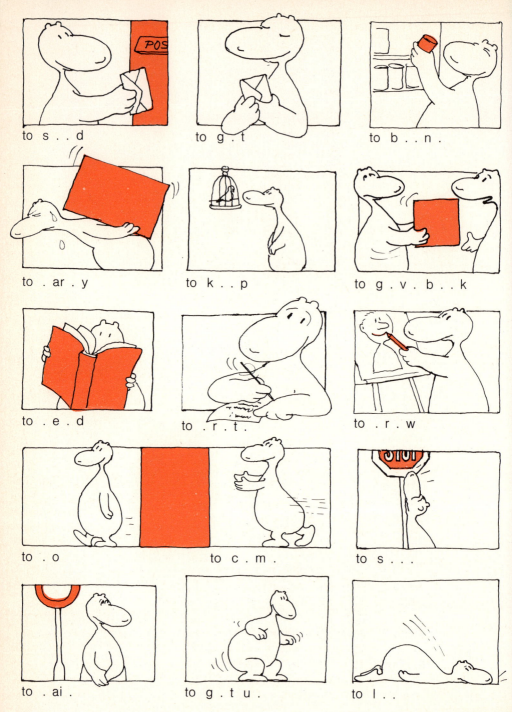

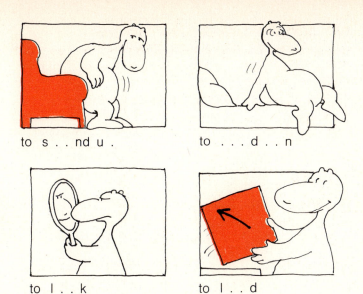

to s..nd u.

to ...d..n

to l..k

to l..d

Part 3 "False friends" (Falsche Freunde)

Es gibt eine Reihe von Verben im Englischen, die eine andere Bedeutung haben, als Du im Deutschen vermuten würdest, sogenannte "false friends".
Zum Beispiel:

1.   **to make – to do**

make heißt herstellen/anfertigen/machen
Example: Mother makes a cake – Mutter stellt einen Kuchen her (backt einen Kuchen).
do heißt   1. tun/verrichten
              2. in Ordnung bringen/erledigen
Example: 1. What are you doing? Was tust Du gerade?
           2. Peter does his homework. Peter erledigt seine Hausaufgaben.

b) Matching exercise – "to make"

Hier sind eine Reihe von Redewendungen mit dem Verb "to make". Ordne die Hälften richtig zu, sieh die Lösung im Lösungsheft nach und lerne die Redewendungen dann auswendig.

to make

1	a coat	C	einen Mantel schneidern	1	C
2	a speech	A	Fratzen schneiden	2	
3	plans	E	eine Rede halten	3	
4	a mistake	B	Krach machen	4	
5	money	F	Pläne machen	5	
6	faces	H	einen Fehler machen	6	
7	a fire	D	telephonieren	7	
8	the bed	G	Geld verdienen	8	
9	a noise	I	das Bett machen	9	
10	a telephone call	J	Feuer anzünden	10	

c) Matching exercise – "to do"

Ordne zu, sieh nach und lerne auswendig!

to do

1	one's best	A	rechnen	1	
2	the washing-up	B	seine Hausaufgaben machen	2	
3	a test	C	60 Meilen schnell fahren	3	
4	right	D	richtig handeln	4	
5	one's homework	E	das Zimmer aufräumen	5	
6	s.b. a favour	F	einen Test schreiben	6	
7	wrong	G	abwaschen	7	
8	the room	H	sein Bestes tun	8	
9	60 miles an hour	I	jemandem einen Gefallen tun	9	
10	sums	J	falsch handeln	10	

d) What a life!

Put in the missing verb forms of "to do" or "to make". Setze die fehlenden Verbformen von "to do" oder "to make" ein.

First Mother has breakfast, then she 1. _____ the rooms and 2. _____ the beds. Later she 3. _____ a little gardening. After that she 4. _____ the shopping. When she has come back to her kitchen she 5. _____ herself a cup of tea and begins to prepare the dinner. When Peter is back from school he 6. _____ his homework. After supper they all 7. _____ the dishes. Mother likes home-made cake, so she usually 8. _____ a cake for the weekend.

e) A dialogue

Fill in do /make
        doing /making

Susan (calling from downstairs): Peter, what are you *doing*?

Peter: I'm _____ my bed.

Susan: But I thought you wanted to _____ a telephone call to Mother in hospital?

Peter: All right. I'll _____ that in a minute.

Susan: And tomorrow you are going to _____ a test. So you have to _____ some work for school.

Peter: O.K. But I haven't got much time to _____ it now. There is a lot of gardening to _____. I've got to help Father first.

f) What you "make" and what you "do"

Überprüfe jetzt, wie gut Du Bescheid weißt. Schreibe in Dein Heft!

the beds – my homework – breakfast – the washing-up – a fire – right – coffee – a test – my best – a noise – a mistake – a telephone call – wrong – the room

Example:

I do ...	I make ...
my homework	the beds

2.

a) to take – to bring

1. "to take" kennzeichnet immer eine Bewegung vom Sprecher weg
= **hin**bringen – **weg**bringen

to take →

Take a letter to the post office.
(Bringe einen Brief zum Postamt)

2. "to bring" kennzeichnet immer eine Bewegung zum Sprecher hin
= **her**bringen – **mit**bringen (zum Sprecher)

to bring ←

Bring me the letter. (Bringe mir den Brief her)
Bring your friends with you. (Bringe Deine Freunde mit)

taking to —————→ **a place**
bringing back from ←

b) Family help

You ask your mother/father what you have to do in the household. Du fragst Deine Mutter/Deinen Vater, was Du im Haushalt helfen kannst. Sie antworten.

Example: <u>Take</u> the parcels <u>to</u> the post office and <u>bring back</u> some postcards.

Forme jetzt ähnliche Sätze nach der Vorlage und schreibe sie in Dein Heft!

take → to   and bring back ←

piece of soap
cups
tools
magazines
parcels
papers
the shirts
black shoes

bathroom
kitchen
your room
shoemaker's
neighbour
post office
cellar

some stamps
some towels
Betty's sandals
Father's hammer
the vacuum cleaner
your schoolbag
some black shoe polish
some postcards

c) Exercise

Put in **take** *or* **bring.**

Father is in the bedroom. He is ill. Peter comes in:

Father: Peter, _____ my plate to the kitchen and _____ a cup of coffee for me, please.
Peter: O.K., Father. Mother is in the sitting-room. Can I _____ her a cup, too?
Father: Yes, of course – but there are my tablets on the bedside table.

Please, _____ them to me. Thank you. Oh, I need some

water. _____ this glass to the bathroom and _____ some water from there.
Peter: All right, Father.

3. Verbs of hearing

1. to hear heißt hören ohne Absicht.
2. to listen (to) heißt (jemandem) bewußt zuhören – lauschen.

Exercise: *Fill in the gaps.* to hear – to listen (to)

1. Don't _____ her, she is a silly goose.

2. We can't _____ what he is saying.

3. I _____ a noise (Geräusch).

4. We _____ but _____ nothing.

4. Verbs of seeing

1. to see heißt sehen, ungewollt wahrnehmen.
2. to look heißt bewußt nach etwas sehen.
3. to watch heißt genau beobachten.

Exercise: *Fill in the gaps.*

1. Blind people cannot _____ .

2. The little girl was _____ at the dolls in the window.

3. Every night father and mother _____ TV.

4. What can you _____ when you _____ out of the window?

5. Verbs of looking / seeing and hearing

to see – sehen (ungewollt wahrnehmen)
to look – bewußt nach etwas sehen
to watch – genau beobachten
to stare at – starr blicken auf/anstarren
to hear – hören ohne Absicht
to listen to – bewußt zuhören/lauschen

Fill in the suitable (geeigneten) verbs of looking/seeing/hearing.

1. He __*hears*__ them talking, but doesn't understand what they are saying.

2. When he is walking through the park, he _____ a bird sing.

3. The little girl has to _____ over the shoulders of the man in front of her to _____ the match.

4. Mother really _____ everywhere but she can't find the purse. (Geldbörse)

5. He _____ quickly over the page.

6. You can't _____ in the dark.

7. Father _____ up from his book, and _____ his brother Jim, whom he has not _____ for years.

8. The boy _____ at the funny dress of the old Lady.

9. When they _____ the noise, they all _____ .

6. The verbs to become / to get
to become heißt **werden** – ganz allgemein.
to get heißt **bekommen/erhalten**.

a) Exercise *Fill in the gaps.*

1. You can _____ apples at the greengrocer's.

2. He has _____ a teacher.

3. Father was very angry when he could not _____ a taxi.

4. My brother wants to _____ a taxi driver when he is big.

5. How much pocket money do you _____ ?

6. Queen Elisabeth II _____ Queen of England in 1952.
(past tense!)

b) Reading Comprehension
Can you become a beefsteak?

Lies die folgende Geschichte sorgfältig durch, unterstreiche die Wörter, die Du nicht verstehst und sieh im Vokabelverzeichnis nach!

A young German has travelled to London by train. He gets off the train at Victoria Station. It has been a long journey and the young German feels very hungry. He goes to a restaurant to have something to eat. It is lunchtime, all the restaurants are full, but then he finds a free seat in one of them. The waiters hurry from table to table to serve the guests. When one of the waiters comes to his table, the German orders a beefsteak. He has to wait a long time for his meal. Half an hour passes – no beefsteak. The young man becomes hungrier and hungrier. When an hour has passed, he shouts in a loud voice: "Waiter, when shall I become a beefsteak?"
"Never, I hope, sir," is the waiter's answer.

c) Questions on the text
Antworte in ganzen Sätzen.

1. Where does the German travel to? _He travels to London_
2. Where does he get off the train? _____
3. Why does he go to a restaurant? _____
4. What does the German order? _____
5. How does he shout? _____
6. What does he shout? _____

7. a) The verb "to go"

to go bedeutet
1. fahren allgemein: The train goes fast.
2. Fahren von Personen mit Fahrzeug: We go to London by car.

Allgemein ist "to go" ein Verb für die verschiedenen Arten der Bewegung.

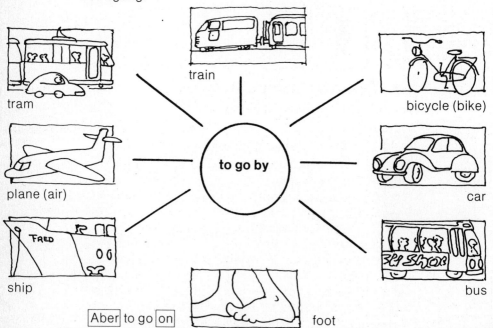

b) How do they get to school?

Peter goes to school by bicycle. – Susan . . Brenda . . Ricky . . David?

  Peter _____

  Susan _____

  Ricky _____

  David _____

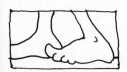  Brenda _____

c) Hobbies and activities

Schreibe die entsprechenden Tätigkeiten in Dein Heft. Diese Liste hilft Dir.

to go skating – to play football – to go skiing – to go shopping – to go fishing – to go swimming – to ride on a horse – to ride on a bike – to go sailing – to dance – to play tennis – to collect stamps

2 AUXILIARIES

Es gibt eine Reihe von Verben, die darauf bestehen, anders als die normalen Verben zu sein. Es sind die sogenannten **Hilfsverben.** Sie werden nur in Verbindung mit einem anderen Vollverb verwendet. (Siehe Seiten 45 ff.) Drei von ihnen – to be / to have / to do – können sich allerdings nicht ganz entscheiden, auf welcher Seite sie stehen sollen. Sie sind einmal Vollverben und dann wieder Hilfsverben, sogenannte **vollständige Hilfsverben,** weil sie alle Formen der Vollverben besitzen, aber meist als Hilfsverb verwendet werden.

Part 1   The verb "to be"

to be →
- **bildet** mit der ing-form (dem present participle) anderer Verben **die Verlaufsform**
- **darf** in Frage und Verneinung **nicht** mit to do gebraucht werden
- **wird** als Vollverb in der Bedeutung von **sein** gebraucht

1.   The forms of "to be"

present tense (Gegenwart)

		English			German	short forms
S I N G U L A R	I	am	a girl	ich bin	ein Mädchen	I'm a girl
	you	are	a boy	du bist	ein Junge	you're a boy
	he	is	German	er ist	Deutscher	he's German
	she	is	English	sie ist	Engländerin	she's English
	it	is	a dog	es ist	ein Hund	it's a dog
P L U R A L	we	are	French	wir sind	Franzosen	we're French
	you	are	Danish	ihr seid	Dänen	you're Danish
	they	are	Dutch	sie sind	Holländer	they're Dutch

	past tense (Vergangenheit)						
	English				German		
S I N G U L A R	I	was	happy	ich	war	glücklich
	you	were	sad	du	warst	traurig
	he	was	careful	er	war	vorsichtig
	she	was	lazy	sie	war	faul
	it	was	bad	es	war	schlecht
P L U R A L	we	were	happy	wir	waren	glücklich
	you	were	sad	ihr	wart	traurig
	they	were	lazy	sie	waren	faul

2. The verb "to be" in the present tense

Trage jeweils die richtige Form von "to be" ein.

1. Henry ___is___ a student.

2. He _____ a good teacher.

3. We _____ busy.

4. You and Mary _____ sisters.

5. The door _____ closed.

6. I _____ tired (müde) now.

7. This _____ a good exercise.

8. Mr. and Mrs. Ashing _____ English.

9. We _____ brothers.

10. I _____ happy.

11. You _____ a good student.

12. She _____ a good friend.

13. Mary and I _____ good friends.

3. The verb "to be" in the past tense
Change the verb to past time and write it in the blanks at the right.
Setze die entsprechende Form von "to be" in der Vergangenheit ein.

1. Richard is in my class.   *was*

2. The weather is good. _____

3. There is someone at the door. _____

4. The windows and doors are open. _____

5. We are good friends. _____

6. I am very hungry. _____

7. Betty and Tom are in the same class. _____

8. This is a good exercise. _____

9. There are many students in our class. _____

10. Mr. Iwen is our English teacher. _____

11. You and Mary are good pupils. _____

12. I am a good student of English. _____

13. Mary and I are also good friends. _____

Part 2   Negation of "to be"

1. Die Formen von "to be" werden mit "not" verneint.
In der Umgangssprache werden meist die "short forms" benutzt.

SINGULAR

present	past tense
I'm not	I wasn't
you aren't	you weren't
he isn't	he wasn't
she isn't	she wasn't
it isn't	it wasn't

PLURAL

present	past tense
we aren't	we weren't
you aren't	you weren't
they aren't	they weren't

2. Mixed exercise

Trage die richtige Form in die Lücken ein.

1. We (am/are) brothers.   *are*

2. Today (is/are) Monday. _____

3. She (isn't/aren't) a good teacher. _____

4. Yesterday Brenda (weren't/wasn't) very busy. _____

5. Mr. Evans (am/is) a teacher. _____

6. I (is/am) a boy. _____

7. The weather (were/was) good yesterday. _____

8. Last year Christmas (wasn't/weren't) very interesting. _____

9. They (was/were) brothers. _____

10. She and Kate (is/are) sisters. _____

11. I (isn't/am not) a teacher of English. _____

12. Paul and I (wasn't/weren't) good friends. _____

3. Answer the questions
Wie man Fragen mit Hilfsverben bildet, s. Seiten 82ff.

1. Are these girls English?   Yes, *they are.*
2. Are you a boy?   Yes, _____
3. Is your friend a boy?   No, *he isn't.*
4. Are you English?   No, _____
5. Were your friends here?   No, _____
6. Is this Mary?   No, _____
7. Is your father 42?   Yes, _____
8. Are they happy?   Yes, _____
9. Was it Peter's ball?   No, _____
10. Was your grandfather a baker?   Yes, _____

Part 3   Hello – Good morning – Goodbye

1.   Sich förmlich begrüßen

Wenn man Leute zum ersten Mal sieht, oder wenn man Lehrer oder andere "Persönlichkeiten" trifft, mit denen man nicht privat zusammen ist, so sagt man:

morgens: Good morning.
nachmittags: Good afternoon.
abends: Good evening.

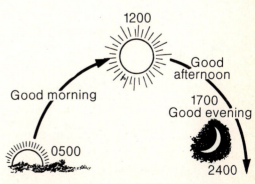

Die Engländer schütteln sich viel seltener die Hände als die Deutschen. Eine Gelegenheit ist, wenn man sich zum ersten Mal trifft – dann sagen beide: "How do you do?"

2. Einen Freund begrüßen und fragen, wie es geht

Kennt man seine Partner schon etwas länger, sieht alles ganz anders aus.

Susan begrüßt Mary und fragt, wie es geht.
Mary antwortet und fragt zurück. Susan geht es nur einigermaßen.

Susan:	Hello, Mary, how are you?
Mary:	I am fine, thanks. And how are you?
Susan:	Well, not too bad.

3. Einen Freund vorstellen

Peter und Susan treffen Mary. Peter und Mary kennen sich noch nicht.

Hello, Susan!   Hello, Mary! This is Peter. He is from London.   Hello, Peter!   Hello, Mary!

4.
Hier sind die Redemittel noch einmal zusammengefaßt.

Redemittel	Redeabsichten
How do you do?	jeden förmlich mit Handschlag begrüßen
Good morning. Good afternoon. Good evening.	jeden förmlich grüßen
Hello, . . .	einen Freund grüßen
This is . . . This is my friend . . .	einen Freund vorstellen
He/she is from . . .	sagen, woher der Freund/die Freundin kommt

5. Im weiteren Gespräch will man mehr über seinen Partner wissen. Man fragt:

Redemittel	Redeabsichten
Are you ... ?	ihn nach seinem Namen fragen
I am ... My name is ... Yes I am. – No, I am not.	darauf antworten
How are you?	ihn fragen, wie es ihm geht
I am fine, thanks. – I am very well, thanks.	antworten, daß es gut geht
Well, not too bad. – Oh, all right.	antworten, daß es nur einigermaßen geht

6. **Zwei Dialoge**

I. Der Lehrer Miller trifft Susan und Peter. Er kennt Peter noch nicht.

Susan: Good morning, Mr. Miller.

Peter: _____

Mr. M.: _____ Susan. _____ ?
Susan: Fine thanks, Mr. Miller.

_____ is Peter. He _____ from London.

Mr. M.: _____ do, Peter.

(They shake hands.)

Peter: _____ do, Mr. Miller.

II. Susan und Peter treffen Mary. Mary kennt Peter nicht.

Mary: _____ Susan.

Susan: _____ Mary.

_____ you?

Mary: Well, _____ (es geht einigermaßen)

Susan: _____ is Peter. He _____ from _____

33

Mary: Hello _____

Peter: _____ Mary.

7. a) Sich verabschieden

Verläßt man am Abend seinen Gesprächspartner, sagt man "Good night". Sage nie "~~Good day~~".

Hier sind verschiedene Möglichkeiten, sich zu verabschieden.

Redemittel	Bemerkungen
Goodbye Bye-bye, Bye See you, See you later	förmlich = "Auf Wiedersehen" nicht förmlich = "Wiedersehen" Verabschiedung von guten Freunden = "Tschüß", "Bis dann", "Bis später".

b) Matching exercise

Zu jeder Redeabsicht gehört eine englische Äußerung. Ordne zu.

1	einen Freund vorstellen	A	He/she is from . . .		
2	jeden förmlich begrüßen	B	How do you do?		
3	jeden fragen, wie es ihr/ihm geht	C	Hello, . . .		
4	förmlich "Auf Wiedersehen" sagen	D	This is . . . This is my friend . . .		
5	jeden förmlich mit Handschlag begrüßen	E	I'm fine, thanks . . .		
6	einen Freund begrüßen	F	I am . . ./My name is . . .		
7	antworten, daß es gut geht	G	See you/see you later		
8	den Namen sagen	I	Goodbye		
9	Verabschiedung von guten Freunden	J	How are you?		
10	sagen, von wo der andere Partner ist	K	Good morning. – Good afternoon.–Good evening.		

Part 4 The "there-structure"

There is – There are – Are there? – Is there?
Mit "there is" oder "there are" drückt man ein örtliches Vorhandensein aus (es befindet sich/es gibt). "There is" wird bei Hauptwörtern in der Einzahl gebraucht, "there are" bei Hauptwörtern in der Mehrzahl. Achtung: Bei der Einleitung mit "there" ändert sich die Wortstellung: an apple is . . . → there is an apple . . .

1. Aussageform

There is	a bike no motor bike	in the basement.	Es befindet sich ein Fahrrad/ kein Motorrad im Keller.
There are	two cars no bikes	in the garage.	Es befinden sich zwei Autos/ keine Fahrräder in der Garage.

2. Frageform

Is there	a bike in the basement?	Yes, there is.
Is there	a motor bike in the basement?	No, there isn't.
Are there	cars in the garage?	Yes, there are.
Are there	bikes in the garage?	No, there aren't.

3. Mixed exercise

I `there is – there are`   II `there isn't – there aren't`
III `is there? – are there?`

I. Aussageform
   Schreibe die Sätze mit den richtigen Formen in Dein Heft und übersetze sie dann.
   1. There (is/are) seven days in a week.
   2. There (is/are) only one chair in this room.
   3. There (is/are) a new student in our class.
   4. There (is/are) two windows in this room.
   5. There (is/are) someone at the door.
   6. There (is/are) a man in the street.

II. Verneinung

Schreibe diese Sätze in der Verneinung in Dein Heft und übersetze sie anschließend.

7. There are many children in the park.
8. There is only one window in this room.
9. There are two doors in this room.
10. There is one new girl in our class.
11. There are two new teachers in our school.
12. There is a policeman on the corner.

III. Frageform

Schreibe die Fragen in Dein Heft und übersetze sie.

13. There are many birds in the tree.
14. There is a mouse in the room.
15. There are twelve months in a year.
16. There is a letter here for you.
17. There is a window in the room.

4. There is -- there are – present tense
Two burglars break into a house
What is Fred saying to Kevin?
Trage ein, was die beiden Einbrecher Fred und Kevin sagen.

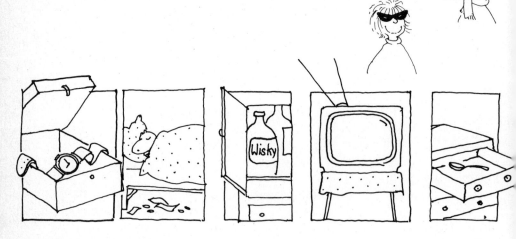

There is _____ There _____ _____ are _____ _____ There _____

in the _____ money _____ _____ _____ silver _____

Some time later the owner of the house, Mr. Carter, and a policeman come.
What are they saying?

Mr. C.: _____

Policem.: _____

Mr. Carter: Is there a watch in the box?
Policeman: No, there isn't.

Mr. C.: _____

Policem.: _____

Mr. C.: _____

Policem.: _____

Mr. C.: _____

Policem.: _____

5. A dialogue

Der Lehrer unterhält sich mit seinen Schülern.
There was – wasn't – were – weren't. Achtung! Vergangenheit!
Fülle die Lücken aus.

Yesterday | there | was | a big football match in town.
Next morning the teacher Mr. Bush is talking to the boys in his class about it.
Mr. Bush: Were you there, Mike?
Mike: No, I wasn't, I was at home.

Mr. Bush: _____, Tom?

Tom: No, _____, I

37

Mr. Bush: What about you, Dave and Kevin?
_____

Dave: No, we _____

Kevin: We _____
_____

Mr. Bush: And you, Richard _____?

Richard: Yes, _____ It _____ very interesting.

6. How to say it?

Is there ... near here?
Du bist fremd in einer Stadt und willst wissen, wo die Orte sind.
Frage nach den Bildern.

$\boxed{-}$ = no $\boxed{+}$ = yes

A: Excuse me, is there a swimming pool near here?
B: Yes, there is a very good swimming pool over there. $\boxed{+}$

A: Excuse me, are there _____ near here?
B: Well, there aren't any discos here. $\boxed{-}$

A: Excuse me, _____?
B: _____ $\boxed{+}$

A: _____ near here?
B: Well, there _____ $\boxed{-}$

A: _____
B: _____ [+]

A: _____
B: _____ [−]

A: _____
B: _____ [−]

Part 5 The verb "to have"

to have
→ bildet die zusammengesetzten Zeiten aller Verben (present perfect/past perfect)
→ darf in Frage und Verneinung in der Regel nicht mit "to do" gebraucht werden
→ wird als Vollverb meist in der Bedeutung von "besitzen" gebraucht

1. The forms of "to have"
present tense – Gegenwart

"to have" wird mit "not" verneint (Kurzform: n't).

		Vollform		Kurzform		Verneinung	
S I N G U L A R	I	have	a car	I've	I	haven't	(have not)
	you	have	a bike	you've	you	haven't	(have not)
	he	has	a book	he's*)	he	hasn't	(has not)
	she	has		she's*)	she	hasn't	(has not)
	it	has		it's*)	it	hasn't	(has not)
P L U R A L	we	have		we've	we	haven't	(have not)
	you	have		you've	you	haven't	(have not)
	they	have		they've	they	haven't	(have not)

*) Vorsicht, diese Kurzformen können auch "he is, she is, it is" heißen. Benutze für das Verb "have" lieber die Vollformen "he has, she has, it has".

past tense – Vergangenheit

	Vollform	Kurzform	Verneinung
SINGULAR I / you / he / she / it	had	'd	hadn't
PLURAL we / you / they			

2. Exercise – "to have" – present tense

Fill in the correct form of "to have".

1. I _____ many friends in this class.

2. The dog _____ a long tail.

3. Mrs. Lasins _____ red hair.

4. This room _____ many pictures.

5. Elke and Günther _____ many friends.

6. This book _____ a green cover.

7. We _____ pencils but no pens.

8. I _____ a new pair of trousers.

9. You _____ a good bike.

10. David _____ two sisters but no brother.

11. I _____ grey eyes.

12. The teacher _____ a bad cold today.

3. **"have" in der Bedeutung von "haben/besitzen"**
Es wird in der Umgangssprache meist mit dem Wort "got" gebraucht: "have got/has got".
What have the children got? Was besitzen die Kinder?
Schreibe auf, was die Kinder haben und was nicht.
Beispiel: Jim has got a bike but he hasn't got a motorbike.

Susan _____ but _____

Peter _____ but _____

Fred _____ but _____

The dog _____ but _____

Father & Mother _____

_____ but they _____

Dolly and Molly _____

_____ but _____

4. My family

Brenda erzählt über ihre Familie.
Setze die entsprechenden Formen von "to be" und "to have" ein.

0. My name is Brenda.

1. I _____ 10 years old.

2. I _____ a sister.

3. She _____ seven years old.

4. Her name _____ Kitty.

5. My brothers _____ 21 and 16 years old.

6. They _____ a car and a motor bike.

7. My father _____ a teacher.

8. My mother _____ a housewife.

9. She _____ 30 years old and looks very pretty.

10. I _____ a friend, too.

11. He _____ a new bike.

12. And we _____ a lot of fun playing in the park.

Part 6 The verb "to do"

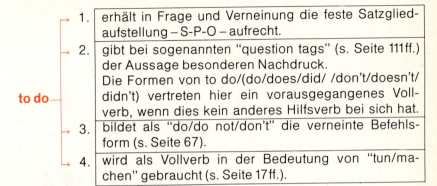

to do
1. erhält in Frage und Verneinung die feste Satzgliedaufstellung – S-P-O – aufrecht.
2. gibt bei sogenannten "question tags" (s. Seite 111ff.) der Aussage besonderen Nachdruck. Die Formen von to do/(do/does/did/ /don't/doesn't/didn't) vertreten hier ein vorausgegangenes Vollverb, wenn dies kein anderes Hilfsverb bei sich hat.
3. bildet als "do/do not/don't" die verneinte Befehlsform (s. Seite 67).
4. wird als Vollverb in der Bedeutung von "tun/machen" gebraucht (s. Seite 17ff.).

1. The forms of "to do"

Achtung: Auch "to do" wird mit "to do" verneint.

present tense — **Verneinung**

SINGULAR				
	I	do	my homework	don't do my homework
	you	do	your homework	don't do your homework
	he / she / it	**does**	his / her / its homework	**doesn't do** his / her / its homework

PLURAL				
	we	do	our homework	don't do our homework
	you	do	your homework	don't do your homework
	they	do	their homework	don't do their homework

past tense — **Verneinung**

SINGULAR				
	I	did	my homework	didn't do my homework
	you	did	your homework	didn't do your homework
	he / she / it	did	his / her / its homework	didn't do his / her / its homework

PLURAL				
	we	did	our homework	didn't do our homework
	you	did	your homework	didn't do your homework
	they	did	their homework	didn't do their homework

Die Vollform für die Verneinung heißt **do not/does not** und **did not**.

2. Do/does

A lot of questions! (Fragefürwörter siehe Seite 94f.).
Setze "do/does" ein.

1. Where __*do*__ you live?

2. Where _____ Mary live?

3. What time _____ you arrive at school every day?

4. How well _____ John speak English?

5. How _____ you feel today?

6. How often _____ it rain during the month of April?

7. Why _____ they work so hard?

8. Where _____ Mary and her sister live?

3 DEFECTIVE AUXILIARIES

Die unvollständigen Hilfsverben sind deshalb unvollständig (defective), weil sie nicht alle Zeiten bilden können.
Sie drücken auch meist keinen selbständigen Begriff aus, sondern bezeichnen nur die Art und Weise eines Vollverbs näher.
Sie werden deshalb nur in Verbindung mit einem anderen Vollverb verwendet.

Part 1   Vocabulary

1.   Here are some of the defective auxiliaries.

a) | can – cannot – can't
(nicht) können
[kæn, 'kænɔt, kɑ:nt] | drückt **geistige** und **körperliche Fähigkeit** aus
I can swim.
He can speak English but he cannot/can't speak French.

b) | could/couldn't könnte
(nicht) [kud, 'kudnt] | kann als **höfliche Frage** benutzt werden
Could you help me, please?

c) | must – müssen
[mʌst] | drückt ein **notwendiges Müssen** aus
You must learn your English words.
(Du mußt Deine englischen Vokabeln lernen.)

d) | mustn't – nicht dürfen
['mʌsnt] | drückt ein **Verbot** aus
You mustn't talk so much.
(Du darfst nicht so viel reden.)

e) | need – brauchen
    [ni:d] | drückt **Notwendigkeit** aus
Need I tell you more? (Brauche ich mehr zu sagen?/Mehr brauche ich wohl nicht zu sagen.)

f) | needn't – nicht brauchen
    ['ni:dnt] | drückt eine **Verneinung** der **Notwendigkeit** aus
You needn't work so hard.
(Du brauchst nicht so hart zu arbeiten.)

g) | may – may not dürfen
    (nicht) [mei] | drückt eine **Erlaubnis** aus
May I go out? Yes, you may.
(Darf ich rausgehen? Ja, du darfst.)

h) | will [wil] – wollen
    would [wud] – würden | drücken eine **Bitte** oder einen **Wunsch** aus
Will/Would you help me please?
(Würden Sie mir bitte helfen?)

3. Merke:

Unvollständige Hilfsverben

| haben | kein s | in der 3. Person der Gegenwart | → | He can swim.
She mu**stn**'t come in. |

| werden | in Frage und Verneinung **nicht** mit to do umschrieben (wie die Vollverben) | → → | May I **go** out?
You **cannot** fly. |

| haben | die Grundform eines Vollverbs ohne 'to' nach sich | → → | She **can speak** English.
We **may go.** |

Part 2 Fragestellung mit Hilfsverben

1. How to ask questions?

Hier ist ein Aussagesatz:

subject	predicate		object
	auxiliary	full verb	
Peter	**can**	understand	English

Sieh Dir den Satz einmal genau an. Zu welchem Satzteil gehört das Hilfsverb "can"?

Richtig! Zum Teil des Prädikats. Es ist ein Hilfsverb.
Nun sieh Dir die Frageform an!

	S	P	O	
	subject	predicate	object	
	Peter	**can** understand	English	Aussagesatz
Can	Peter	understand	English?	Fragesatz

Was ist passiert? Bei der Fragebildung von Sätzen mit Hilfsverben, z. B. can – may – must – could etc., rückt das Hilfsverb meist an den Anfang des Satzes vor das Subjekt. Das Vollverb bleibt in der Grundform, wo es ist.

Die Umschreibung mit "to do" wird dann **nicht** angewendet, weil die Satzstellung S – P – O sich ja nicht ändert. Hilfsverb + Subjekt + Prädikat + Objekt ist die Reihenfolge der Satzglieder im Fragesatz, wenn ein Hilfsverb wie z. B. can – may – must – etc. im Satz vorkommt. Auch in der Frageform steht das Hauptverb immer in der Grundform ohne "to".

	Hilfsverb	S	P	O
I	Can	you	see	the thief?
II	Must	we	do	our homework?
III	Could	they	open	the window?
IV	May	Peter	ride	his bike?

2. *Change to question form. Bilde Fragesätze.*
Schreibe auch das Hauptverb des Satzes mit.

1. He can swim very well. _Can he swim very well_ ?

2. They may sit here. _____ ?

3. I can understand everything. _____

_____ ?

4. She can meet us after breakfast. _____

_____ ?

5. You may smoke here. _____ ?

6. We will be back at 3 o'clock. _____ ?

7. He must do that again. _____ ?

8. Peter can play the piano. _____ ?

9. The teacher could do it very well. _____

_____?

10. She will telephone us later. _____

3. Hier ist eine schwierigere Übung.
Bilde Fragen aus den Wörtern und schreibe sie in Dein Heft.

must   French   can   Sheila   my hands   work   do

ride   must   the cooking   may   you   wash   a bike

every   workday   Father

can   Mother   I   speak

Example

auxiliary verb	subject	verb	object
can	Sheila	speak	French

4. ### Fragestellung mit dem Hilfsverb "to be" (sein)
Das gleiche Schema gilt auch für Sätze, die eine Form von "to be" als Verb oder Teil eines Verbs haben.

	The book	is	on the table		Aussagesatz
Is	the book		on the table?		Fragesatz

oder

	The boy	is	reading	a book	Aussagesatz
Is	the boy		reading	a book?	Fragesatz

5. Exercise

Write down the sentences and form the questions.
Schreibe die Sätze auf und stelle die Fragen.

1. | My | is | garage | father | in | the |

   My father is in the garage.

   Question: *Is my father in the garage?* ?

2. | The | is | cat | walking | wall | the | on |

   _____

   Question: _____ ?

3. | Mother | windows | cleaning | the | is |

   _____

   Question: _____ ?

4. | The | are | in | playground | playing | children | the |

   _____

   Question: _____ ?

5. | The | are | round | running | the | lions | cage |

   _____

   Question: _____ ?

6. | The | getting | bus | boys | are | the | on |

   _____

   Question: _____ ?

Bei der Fragebildung von Sätzen rückt das Hilfsverb meist an den Anfang des Satzes vor das Subjekt – wie im Deutschen –, wenn

| ein Hilfsverb wie can – must – may – could im Prädikat steht | **oder** | das Prädikat eine Form von "be" ist oder im Prädikat eine Form von "be" vorkommt. |

6. Hier mußt Du ganz besonders aufpassen. Finde die Fragen, die auf die Antworten passen. Die angegebenen Wörter müssen in der Frage vorkommen.

1. German/is/she _____? Yes, she is.

2. Peter Tode/are/you *Are you* _____? No, I am not.

3. Father/football/is/playing _____? No, he isn't.

4. the window/open/is _____? Yes, it is.

5. I/go/out/may _____? Yes, you may.

6. Sheila/write/a letter/must _____? No, she mustn't.

7. the boys/working/garden/are/in _____? No, they aren't.

Part 3 Negation – Verneinung mit Hilfsverben

Ganz einfach ist die Sache, wenn der Satz ein Hilfsverb oder eine Form von "to be" enthält – also

| can | may | must | could | is | are | was | were |

In diesem Fall wird einfach das Wörtchen | not | gebraucht. | Not | steht unmittelbar | hinter | dem Hilfsverb oder der Form von "to be".

can + not werden in einem Wort geschrieben: **cannot**
will + not werden **won't** geschrieben.

1. Fill in the correct forms of the auxiliaries.

| − | = verneint | + | = bejaht

subject	predicate		object	Hilfsverb	
0. grandmother	*cannot*	play	football	−	can
1. the girls	_____	bake	a cake	+	must
2. lions	_____	read	books	−	can
3. yesterday Brian	_____	play	with his friends	−	could

50

4. Mr. Black	_____	play	cricket	−	must
5. cats	_____	make	ice-cream	−	can
6. the children	_____	listening	to records	−	be
7. Mother	_____	cleaning	the rooms	+	be

2. Change to negative form

Schreibe das Hilfsverb mit "not" und das Hauptverb des Satzes in die Lücken.

1. Father must see her. *must not see*

2. I can telephone him later. _____

3. You can speak English well. _____

4. She would wait outside. _____

5. Henry may go to the party. _____

6. We must tell Father about it. _____

7. He can swim very well. _____

8. You may wait in the office. _____

9. I hope she will come back soon. _____

10. He said he would come. _____

Für die Verneinung bei Sätzen mit Hilfsverben braucht man:

1. das Wort "not"   Mother cannot speak English.
                      The sun is not shining.

   dazu muß kommen

2. ein Hilfsverb – can – may – must – will – could etc. – oder
   eine Form von "to be" (am – are – is – was – were)

Das Wort "not" steht unmittelbar **hinter** dem Hilfsverb oder der Form von "to be".

Ist im Satz ein Hilfsverb, so steht das Hauptverb immer in der Grundform ohne "to".

Part 4 Das Hilfsverb can – can't – could

Das Hilfsverb "can" drückt eine geistige oder körperliche Fähigkeit oder Unfähigkeit aus.

1. What can't you do? (Was kannst Du nicht tun?)
Bilde Sätze und schreibe sie in Dein Heft.
Example: You can't buy without money. (Du kannst nicht ohne Geld einkaufen.)

You can't	buy things / cut / sweep the floor / hear / smell / taste		tongue / chalk / ears / nose / key / comb
	write on the blackboard	without (a) (ohne)	money
	knock in nails / wipe things / lock doors / comb your hair / see		knife / broom / hammer / cloth / eyes

2. A holiday camp
Say what you can do and what you can't do.

1. I can *ride on a horse.*

3. I can _____

2. I can _____

4. I can't _____

5. I can _____

7. I can't _____

6. I can't _____

8. I can't _____

3. Lost in the woods

Peter and Mary are lost (haben sich verirrt.)
Fill in the dialogue!

Peter: Mary, where are you?

Mary: Here, _____ you hear me?

Peter: Yes, but I _____ hear you very well.
You are very far away.

Mary: _____ you see me?

Peter: No, I _____. There are too many trees.
Mary: I'm coming nearer to you.

I _____ hear you better now.

Peter: But I still _____ see you.
Mary: No?
Peter and Mary: Ouch!

4. Mother is ill in bed

You must help with the housekeeping. Your friends are downstairs and want to play with you.
Deine Freunde wollen mit Dir die verschiedenen Aktivitäten machen. Du mußt aber Deiner Mutter helfen!

Fülle die Lücken aus und schreibe die Sätze anschließend in Dein Heft.

Example:

Your friends: You:
Come on. Let's go ...

1	to the beach		Sorry, I can't. I must make the beds.	A
2	sailing		Sorry, I can't.	B
3	to the zoo		Sorry,	C
4	to the football match			D
5	out			E
6	swimming			F
7	to the park			G

5. Could – könnte (konnte)

Die Vergangenheit von "can" heißt "could".
"Could" wird aber auch als Verb der höflichen Bitte gebraucht – "könnte".

Fülle die Dialogrollen aus. $\boxed{+}$ = bejaht $\boxed{-}$ = verneint

use
A) I'm late! Could I use your bike?
B) Yes, of course. $\boxed{+}$

take
A) It's raining. Could I _____ your _____ ?
B) Yes, you can. $\boxed{+}$

meet
A) Mary is at the station? _____ her?
B) No, _____ $\boxed{-}$

use
A) I'm tired. _____ your _____ ?
B) _____ $\boxed{+}$

use
A) I want to play tennis. _____ racket?
B) _____ $\boxed{+}$

55

6. Could – would

Bilde Sätze mit den Verben der höflichen Bitte (verbs of request). Sieh noch einmal bei den Vollverben nach. Dann schreibe in Dein Heft.

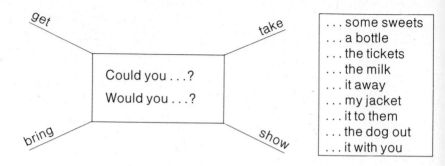

Example: Could you take the milk to the kitchen, please?

7. Mixed exercise

What about your English?
Beantworte jetzt die Fragen über Deine Englischkenntnisse.

Yes, I can./No, I can't.

1. Can you ask for a word in English that you don't know? _____
2. Can you ask questions? _____
3. Can you tell me what you did yesterday? _____
4. Can you tell me what you are doing at this moment? _____
5. Can you write a letter or a postcard in English? _____
6. Do you like listening to English and American songs? _____
7. Can you understand spoken English? _____

Part 5 How to say it

1. Asking for help (Bitten um Hilfeleistung)
Setze die Antwort ein und benutze die Redemittel.

Can you shut the door, please?

die Bitte akzeptieren

_____

Can you open the window?

um Aufschub bitten

_____

Can you take this book to Mary, please?

um Aufschub bitten

_____

Can you show me your homework?

die Bitte akzeptieren, einverstanden sein

_____

Redemittel

Just a moment, please.
(Einen Augenblick, bitte.)

Yes, all right.
(Ja, in Ordnung.)

All right, I'll do it.
(Ja, ich will es tun.)

OK.
(In Ordnung.)

In a minute.
(Gleich./Sofort.)

2. What to say in the classroom
Was sage ich, wenn ...

| ich etwas nicht verstehe? | I can't understand that. I'm sorry, I don't understand. |

| ich Hilfe brauche? | Help! Can you help me? I need some help. |

| ich etwas nicht richtig sehen kann? | I can't see very well. I can't see the picture. The picture is upside down. |

| ich etwas wiederholt haben möchte? | Please say that again. Can you say that once more, please? |

| ich nicht weiß, was ein englisches Wort bedeutet? | What's the meaning of ....? What does .... mean? |

| ich mit der Arbeit fertig bin? | I've finished, please come here. I'm ready. Please have a look at my worksheet. |

| ich etwas zu schwierig finde? | I can't do it. It's too difficult. What have I got to do? |

| ich wissen will, wie etwas geschrieben wird? | Can you write that word on the board? How do you spell that word? |

4 TRAFFIC

Part 1   Vocabulary

1.   What is it?
Fill in. This list will help you.:
aeroplane – taxi – train – bicycle (bike) – car – tricycle – lorry – caravan – bus (double-decker) – motor cycle (bike) – van – tractor – hovercraft – tram

2. Crossword puzzle
Fill in.

Part 2 Traffic signs (Verkehrszeichen)

When you are in England, you must be very careful in the streets because all the traffic moves on the left.

Before you cross a street you must look to the right first and then to the left.

It's better to cross a street at a crossing where there are traffic lights. But wait for green, don't cross the street at amber or red.

1. Traffic light signals

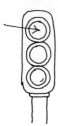 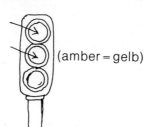 

(amber = gelb)

"Red" means stop. Wait behind the stop line.

"Red and amber" also means stop. Wait until green shows.

"Green" means you may go on.

2. A rhyme

Lerne diesen Vers auswendig und sprich ihn laut.

When the red light shines on top
everybody has to stop.
When the green light shines below (unten)
everybody then can go.
When the light shines amber in the middle
you must wait and guess (raten) the riddle (Rätsel).
Can I start or must I wait?
Hurry up! It's getting late!

3. In the street (Vocabulary)

 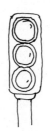 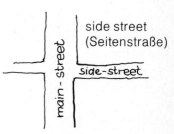

bridge (Brücke)

traffic lights (Verkehrsampel)

main street (Hauptstraße)

zebra crossing
(Zebrastreifen)

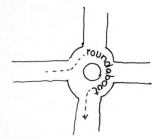

roundabout
(Kreisverkehr)

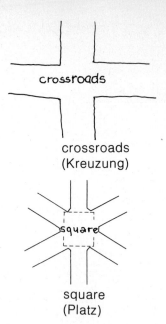

crossroads
(Kreuzung)

square
(Platz)

4. Be careful

In the pictures below you find a number of situations in which the drivers must drive carefully.
Auf den Bildern siehst Du eine Reihe von Situationen, in denen die Fahrer vorsichtig fahren müssen.
"must" heißt "unbedingt müssen" / "mustn't" drückt ein Verbot aus. Siehe auch Seite 45.

The car __mustn't turn__ left.
(not/turn)

It __must turn__ right.
(turn)

The car driver _____ out for the zebra crossing.   (watch)

He _____ the speed.
(slow down)

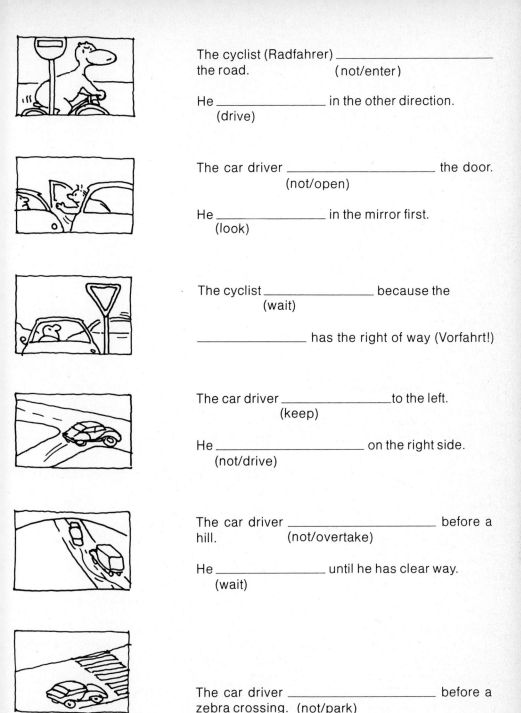

The cyclist (Radfahrer) _____ the road. (not/enter)

He _____ in the other direction. (drive)

The car driver _____ the door. (not/open)

He _____ in the mirror first. (look)

The cyclist _____ because the (wait)

_____ has the right of way (Vorfahrt!)

The car driver _____ to the left. (keep)

He _____ on the right side. (not/drive)

The car driver _____ before a hill. (not/overtake)

He _____ until he has clear way. (wait)

The car driver _____ before a zebra crossing. (not/park)

5. A street scene

Have a look at the picture and write down what the people mustn't do.

1. The driver of the motor bike must slow down the speed because there are people on the zebra crossing.

2. The driver of _____ mustn't open _____.

   He must _____ first.

3. The two _____ mustn't stand and _____ on the _____.

4. The driver of the _____ mustn't *park* before a _____.

5. The girl on _____ hold on to the lorry.

6. Fred _____ let his _____ loose. It _____ run onto the street.

7. The _____ of the sports car _____ overtake the Volkswagen _____ a crossing.

8. The two children _____ ride side by side.

6. Reading comprehension (Leseverstehen)
A strange car (Ein seltsames Auto)

It was eleven o'clock on a very black night and I – a young man – was standing at the top of a hill by the side of a lonely country road trying to get a lift into the nearest town. For an hour I waited but no car came by. At last I saw a car coming very slowly up the hill. It was a very old and dirty car but I was very lucky when it stopped. I got in thankfully. Just at this moment the clock of a nearby church struck midnight and suddenly I noticed that there was no driver in the car. Full of horror I jumped out of the car and ran. When I looked back I saw another man getting into the car. "Don't get in", I shouted, "there's something wrong with that car".
"You are telling me!" shouted the other man. "I've just pushed the car uphill for half a mile!"

Words:
to get a lift – (im Auto) mitgenommen werden
to push – schieben
You are telling me! – Wem sagen Sie das!

Questions

Achtung! Die Geschichte steht in der Vergangenheit. Siehe Seite 147ff. Schreibe die Antworten auf die Fragen in Dein Heft.

1. Did the young man wait long for a lift?
2. What did the young man see at last?
3. What kind of night was it?
4. What time did a car stop?
5. Why did the young man jump out of the car?

5 THE IMPERATIVE

Part 1 Befehlssätze

*Die Befehlsform bezeichnet eine **Aufforderung** oder einen **Befehl** an eine oder mehrere Personen. Sie ist im Englischen für Singular und Plural gleich und wird gebildet aus der Grundform des Verbs ohne "to".*

1. Here is a little rhyme

Lerne das Gedicht auswendig. Unterstreiche die Verben, die in der Befehlsform stehen.

Point to the ceiling (Decke)
Point to the ceiling, point to the floor,
point to the window, point to the door,
clap your hands together one, two, three,
and put your hands on your knee.

2. Bejahter Befehlssatz

	subject	predicate	object	
Aussagesatz	Mother	gives	Peter a glass of milk.	Mutter gibt Peter ein Glas Milch.
Befehlssatz	✗	Give	Peter a glass of milk.	Gib Peter ein Glas Milch!

RULE I Die Befehlsform lautet wie die Grundform des Verbs! Ein Subjekt gibt es nicht!

	subject	predicate	object	
Aussagesatz	Peter and Brenda	make	lunch.	Peter und Brenda machen das Mittagessen.
Befehlssatz	✗	Make	lunch, Peter and Brenda.	Macht das Mittagessen, Peter und Brenda!

RULE II Die Form des Verbs bleibt immer **gleich,** auch wenn **mehrere** Personen angesprochen werden!

Kein Ausrufungszeichen bei den meisten Befehlssätzen, sondern nur bei wirklichen Ausrufen.

| Look out! | | Pay attention! |

RULE III   Bejahte Befehlssätze können durch die Grundform des Verbs "do" verstärkt werden. "Do" wird einfach vor das Verb gestellt.

Sit down.   →   bejahter Befehlssatz
Do sit down.   →   verstärkt

3.   Verneinter Befehlssatz

bejaht	+	**Do** your homework.	**Mache** deine Hausaufgaben!
verneint	−	**Don't play** with your dog.	**Spiele nicht** mit deinem Hund!
bejaht	+	**Go** to school, girls.	**Geht** zur Schule, Mädchen!
verneint	−	**Don't go** to the playground, girls.	**Geht nicht** auf den Spielplatz, Mädchen!

RULE IV   Die verneinte Befehlsform wird in der Einzahl und in der Mehrzahl mit | don't | + | Grundform | gebildet.

4.   Translation exercise

"Go" als Befehlsform kann auf drei verschiedene Arten übersetzt werden:

go — geh (Einzahl)
      geht (Mehrzahl)
      gehen Sie (Anrede)

Wie kannst Du die folgenden Befehlsformen übersetzen:

be quiet   _____   look   _____

listen   _____   don't do that   _____

5. A world tour

You can play on your own or with one or more friends. You need a dice, and a piece for each player. The players throw the dice in turn. You may move forward as many squares as the number on the dice. Follow the instructions in the squares. The winner is the first one to reach the finish (25).

Du kannst alleine spielen oder mit einem oder mehreren Freunden. Du brauchst einen Würfel und für jeden Mitspieler einen Stein. Gewürfelt wird reihum, Du kannst so viele Felder vorrücken, wie der Würfel Augen zeigt. Beachte die Anweisungen auf den Feldern. Sieger ist, wer zuerst am Ziel (25) ist.

6. Befehlsformen bei mehreren Personen

Wenn man eine Person oder mehrere Personen auffordert, mit einem selbst zusammen etwas zu tun, so beginnt man diese Aufforderung mit "Let's ..." = "Laß(t) uns ...".

Schreibe die Aufforderung neben die Bilder, benutze die Verben play – go to – make – read – listen to – look at.

1. *Let's play some records.*

2. *Let's go*

3. _____

4. _____

5. _____

6. _____

7. _____

8. _____

Part 2   Parts of the body – Körperteile

1. Vocabulary

Look at Fred and answer the questions about parts of the body!

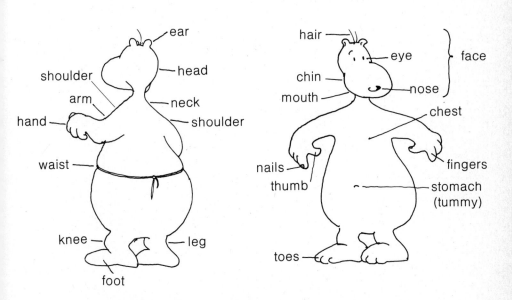

It's between your head and your body.   *neck*

They are at the ends of your fingers.   _____

It's between your nose and your chin.   _____

They are on both sides of the head.   _____

It's below your eyes and above your mouth.   _____

They are between your body and your feet.   _____

They are at the top ends of your arms.   _____

You walk on them.   _____

2. What is it?

Fülle die Lücken aus.

1. It's on your neck.
It's your _____

2. You can smell with it.
It's your _____

3. You can speak with it.
It's your _____

4. You can hear with them.
They are your _____

5. Its colour can be brown, grey, black, red or fair.
It's _____

6. You have five _____
_____ on each _____

7. You have one _____
on each _____

8. You can see with them.
They are your _____

3. Parts of the body – Mixed exercise

Put the right word into the right place.

1. The little boy rides on his father's _____.
(shoulders/nose)

2. The neck is between the _____ and the _____.
(chest/hands/ears/head)

3. The girl with the long _____ runs very fast. (toes/legs)

4. Little Brenda eats too much cake, now her _____ hurts (schmerzt). (leg/tummy)

5. The neighbour wears a hat on his _____. (ears/head)

6. The old gentleman has grey _____. (knees/hair)

7. The teacher says: put your _____ up.   (hands/face)

8. It's winter time and cold. Betty runs home.

She has a red _____.   (tummy/nose)

9. Mother has very good _____. She hears very well.
(feet/ears)

10. Wash your _____ before you eat.   (hair/hands)

11. Father has good _____, he can see the little bird.
(toes/eyes)

12. Hazel plays the guitar with her _____.   (fingers/feet)

4. ## Keep fit with Fred

Sieh Dir die Bilder an und lerne die Kommandos für Freds Turnübungen auswendig.

stand up   sit down   lift your left foot   touch your nose

jump up and down   lift your left arm   touch your head   lie down

5. Give orders

Tell your friend Fred what to do.
to put – to jump – to touch – to lie – to bend – to lift – to stand.
Verwende die Befehlsform und schreibe in Dein Heft.

6 ASKING THE WAY – TELLING THE WAY – FINDING THE WAY

Part 1   Buildings in a town

Sieh Dir das Bild an und ordne den Bezeichnungen Nummern zu.

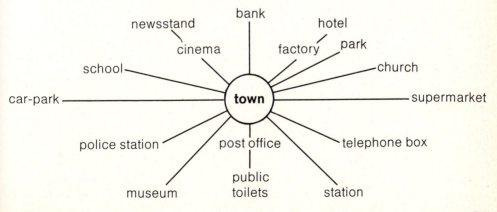

Part 2   How to tell the way / How to ask the way

1.   Matching exercise

Ordne die Redemittel den Zeichnungen zu.

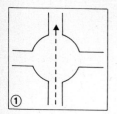

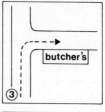
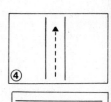
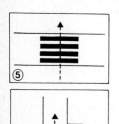
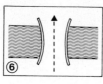

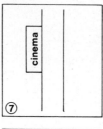

A	The cinema is on the left.	B	Go across the square.	C	Go past the cinema.
D	Go as far as the traffic lights.	E	Go straight on.	F	Turn left into Queen Street.
G	Go across the bridge.	H	Go across the zebra crossing.	I	Go along King Street.
J	Turn right at the butcher's.	K	Take the second road on the left.		

Fill in:

1	2	3	4	5	6	7	8	9	10	11

2. How to ask the way

Nach dem Weg kannst Du so fragen:

Excuse me,
can you tell
me the way to
King Street?

Entschuldigen Sie,
können Sie mir den Weg
zur King Street sagen?

Could you please
tell me how to get
to King Street?

Können Sie mir bitte sagen,
wie ich zur King Street
komme?

Excuse me,
would you mind
telling me the way
to King Street, please?

Entschuldigen Sie bitte,
würde es Ihnen etwas
ausmachen, mir den Weg
zur King Street zu erklären?

Straßennamen haben im Englischen meist keinen Artikel.

3.
Wenn Du den Weg nicht weißt, kannst Du es so sagen:

1. I'm sorry, I don't know. (Es tut mir leid, ich weiß es nicht.)
2. I'm a stranger here myself. (Ich bin selbst fremd hier.)
3. Sorry, I can't help you. (Es tut mir leid, ich kann dir/Ihnen nicht helfen.)

4.
Wenn Du die Frage nicht verstanden hast, mußt Du nachfragen:

1. Pardon? — Wie bitte?
2. King Street? — King Street?
3. The way to King Street? — Den Weg zur King Street?
4. I'm sorry, I didn't get you. — Entschuldigen Sie bitte, ich habe Sie nicht verstanden.

5. Telling the way

Eine Wegbeschreibung muß klar und einfach sein. Die folgenden Angaben können dazu eine Hilfe sein:

1. Auffallende Merkmale	= park – church – post office etc.
2. Entfernungsangaben	= about ... metres – miles – kilometres from ...
3. Zählung von Straßen	= the fourth street – the third traffic light.
4. Richtungsangaben	= turn left/right – drive past – along – across – through – straight on etc.

6. A dialogue

Lies den Dialog laut vor.

A. Excuse me.
B. Yes.
A. Could you please tell me how to get to the church?
B. Yes, go straight on as far as the traffic lights.
   The church is on the left.
A. Thank you.

7. Lost – Verirrt

Peter and Brenda are walking along Market Street. They want to go to the station but they can't find their way.

They are lost!

Fill in!

Brenda: Left? Right? Oh!!
Peter, we are lost. Let's ask the policeman over there.

Peter: Excuse me, can you _____ me

_____ to the station?

Policeman: Yes, of course. Go straight _____ as

far as the _____ lights. Turn _____ into King Street

and go _____ . Turn _____ at the post office. Walk

_____ the police station on your left and then turn

_____ into Station Road. The station is the big building on your right.

8. Telling the way

Dies ist ein Bild einer englischen Kleinstadt, in der Du gerade zu Gast bist. Du kennst Dich schon hervorragend aus und beschreibst auf englisch den Weg von der Kirche zur Bank.

1. Go _____ past the _____ shop till you come to the _____ _____ box.

2. _____ right at the _____.

3. Go _____ past the super_____ on your _____.

4. _____ the street at the cinema.

5. Then _____ left at the next _____.

6. The bank is on your _____ on the other _____ of the street.

9. How to say it

Hier sind die Redemittel noch einmal zusammengefaßt.

1.

Go	up	King Rd. (Road)	sagen, daß man die Königstraße raufgehen soll
Walk	down	King St. (Street)	sagen, daß man die Königstraße runtergehen soll
Drive	down	King Ave. (Avenue)	sagen, daß man die Königsallee runterfahren soll
Go		straight on.	sagen, daß man geradeaus gehen soll

2.

	King Road		traffic lights.	sagen, daß man die Königstraße an der Ampel überqueren soll
Cross	King Street	at the	next corner.	sagen, daß man die Königstraße an der nächsten Ecke überqueren soll
	King Avenue		second corner.	sagen, daß man die Königsallee an der zweiten Ecke überqueren soll

3.

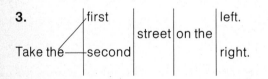

Take the	first	street	on the	left.	sagen, daß man die erste Straße links gehen soll
	second			right.	sagen, daß man die zweite Straße rechts gehen soll

4.

(Then)	turn	left	at the	first	corner.	sagen, daß man an der ersten Ecke nach links gehen muß
		right		third	traffic light.	sagen, daß man an der dritten Ampel nach rechts gehen muß

5.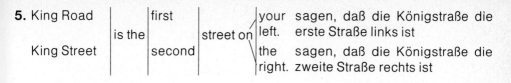

King Road		first		your	sagen, daß die Königstraße die
	is the		street on	left.	erste Straße links ist
King Street		second		the right.	sagen, daß die Königstraße die zweite Straße rechts ist

6.

The school		left.	sagen, daß die Schule auf der linken Seite ist
	is on your		
The hospital		right.	sagen, daß das Krankenhaus auf der rechten Seite ist

7. It's at the end of King Street.   sagen, daß die gesuchte Straße am Ende der Königstraße ist

They are at the other end of King Street.   sagen, daß die ... am anderen Ende der Königstraße sind

8. Sorry, I don't know.   sagen, daß man es nicht weiß

9. Over there.   sagen, daß etwas dort drüben ist

It's over there.   zeigen, wo etwas ist,

They are over there.   und sagen: da drüben.

7 HOW TO ASK QUESTIONS

Part 1   ***Die Umschreibung mit – do/does/did – bei Sätzen mit Vollverben***

Während sich im Deutschen die Frageform von der Aussageform durch eine andere Reihenfolge der Wörter unterscheidet,

Beispiel | Du | siehst | die Frau | | Siehst | Du | die Frau? |
          | S | P | O | | P | S | O |
          | Aussagesatz | | Fragesatz |

ist dies im Englischen **nicht** möglich, sondern die Frageform wird – ebenso wie die Verneinung (s. Seite 89 ff.) – durch Umschreibung mit – do/does/did – gebildet.

Die Hilfszeitwörter "can – may – must – could – will" etc. werden **nicht** mit "do/does/did" umschrieben (s. Seite 45 ff.).

Bevor wir weitergehen, sehen wir uns die Formen von "to do" noch einmal an.

1.   Forms of "to do"

present tense – Gegenwart

Bejahung   Verneinung

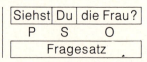

Die Langform für die Verneinung heißt **do not**

Frageform   verneinte Frage

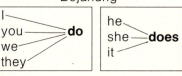      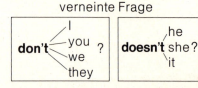

2. Wie bildet man nun die Frage?

Sieh Dir diesen Aussagesatz an.
Wie Du weißt, ist die Reihenfolge der Satzglieder im Englischen immer gleich!

"Football players	play	football"
Subjekt +	Verb +	Objekt
S +	P +	O

Damit diese Satzstellung auch im Fragesatz erhalten bleibt, nimmt die englische Sprache "do" oder "does" zu Hilfe (in der Gegenwart; "did" in der Vergangenheit).

	subject	verb	object	
	Football players	play	football.	Aussagesatz
Do	football players	play	football?	Fragesatz

Das Verb "to do" hilft also, die englische Satzstellung zu erhalten; deshalb der Name **Hilfsverb**.

Diese Hilfestellung nennt man auch "Umschreibung".
Warum muß die Umschreibung mit "to do" in Fragesätzen angewendet werden?

Damit die _____ erhalten bleibt!

3. Exercise:

Setze die Umschreibung mit "to do" ein.

1. Cats eat fish.   *Do cats eat fish?*

2. You speak English.   _____

3. Peter and Brenda smoke. _____

4. Cats drink milk.   _____

5. I know my headmaster.   _____

6. You often go to the cinema. _____

7. They live on the second floor. _____

8. Teachers mark tests.   _____

9. Pilots fly planes.   _____

10. We play tennis every summer.   _____

11. Children like sweets.   _____

4.   Die Umschreibung mit "to do" in der 3. Person Einzahl

Hier ist noch eine Besonderheit, die sehr wichtig ist!
Sieh Dir diesen Aussagesatz an:

	S	P	O	
	Betty	help**s**	Mother.	Aussagesatz
Does	Betty	help	Mother?	Fragesatz

Das "-s" der 3. Person (Betty/she) wandert bei der Umschreibung mit "to do" an den Anfang des Satzes. Aus "do" wird dann "does". Das **Verb** selbst steht immer in der **Grundform** und hat dann nie eine Endung "-s" der 3. Person.

Die Antwort auf eine solche Frage kann heißen:

Yes, he/she/it **does**.   No, he/she/it **doesn't**.

5.   Exercise:

Stelle die Fragen und beantworte sie sinngemäß.

Peter	likes	sport.	Does	he	play	football?	*Yes, he does.*
Jacho	is	a monkey.	Does	it	eat	bananas?	*Yes,*
Brenda	is	a pupil.	Does	she	go	to work?	*No,*
Mr. Black	is	a pilot.	____	he	fly	planes?	
John	helps	his father in the garden.	____	he	sell	things?	
A cow	eats	grass.	____	it	like	eggs?	

6. Mixed exercise

Do/does. Ask questions and mark with a cross. Kreuze an und stelle dann die Frage.

Statement	Do	Does	Question
1. Mary gets up at a quarter to seven.		X	Does Mary get up at a quarter to seven?
2. She goes to the bathroom.		X	Does she
3. Her mother makes the breakfast.			
4. Father and Jimmy come down from the bedroom.			
5. The dog barks in the garden.			
6. Jimmy opens the door and goes into the garden.			
7. Peter, Brenda and Susan wait at the gate.			
8. They all go to school.			
9. It snows in winter.			
10. Jack remembers him.			
11. He speaks English very clearly.			
12. John smokes very much.			
13. We come to class on time.			
14. Your father plays football.			
15. I wash my face every morning.			

7. Billy and Brenda are talking about school

Fill in do/does, don't.

Billy: _____ you like to go to school?

Brenda: Yes, I do.

Billy: _____ learn English at school?

Brenda: No, _____.

Brenda: _____ your teacher speak German?

Billy: Yes, he _____.

Billy: _____ your teacher drink milk during the lesson?

Brenda: No, _____.

Brenda: _____ your teacher read newspapers during the lesson?

Billy: _____, he _____.

Billy: _____ your parents help you with your homework?

Brenda: Yes, _____.

Billy: _____ you and your friends like geography?

Brenda: No, _____.

8. A quiz

Du kennst doch sicher das Ratespiel "Begrifferaten". Der eine Partner denkt sich einen Gegenstand, der andere versucht, durch Fragen diesen Gegenstand zu erraten.
Read the dialogue and guess the thing.

John: I'm thinking of a thing.
Susan: Can I see it here?
John: No, you can't.
Susan: Do people have it in the house?
John: Yes, they have.

Susan: Do we eat it? — John: No, we don't.

Susan: Can I write with it? — John: No, you can't.

Susan: Does one smoke it? — John: No, one doesn't.

Susan: Is the thing in the sitting-room? — John: Yes, it is.

Susan: Do I use it every day? — John: Yes, you do.

Susan: Is it a piece of furniture? — John: Yes, it is.

Susan: Can I lie on it? — John: No, you can't.

Susan: Can I sit on it? — John: Yes, you can.

Susan: It's a _____ then. — John: Yes, it is.

9. Defective dialogue

Now it's your turn.
This time you ask the questions!
Jetzt stellst Du die Fragen! Achte auf die Verben in den Antworten.
Sie sagen Dir, mit welchen Verben Du die Fragen einleiten mußt.

You: Ask him if you can see it here:

Can I see it here? _____ John: No, you can't.

You: Ask him if we use it every day:

Do we _____? John: Yes, we do.

You: Ask him if we eat it.

Do _____? John: No, we don't.

You: Ask him if you can hold it in your hand.

Can I _____? John: Yes, you can.

You: Ask him if one writes with it.

_____? John: No, one doesn't.

You: Ask him if you have it in the house.

Have I got _____? John: Yes, you have.

You: Ask him if it is in the kitchen.

_____? John: No, it isn't.

You: Ask him if it is a toilet article.

_____? John: Yes, it is.

You: Ask him if you wash your face with it.

_____ I _____? John: No, you don't.

You: Ask him if you brush your teeth with it.

_____? John: No, you don't.

You: Ask him if you can comb your hair with it.

_____? John: Yes, you can.

You: Ask him if it is a comb.

_____? John: Yes, it is!

8 NEGATION

Part 1   Verneinung mit einer Form von "to do"

Sätze, in denen weder eine Form von "to be" noch ein Hilfsverb vorkommen, bilden die Verneinung mit der Umschreibung durch "to do".

Bilde nie die Verneinung eines Satzes einfach mit not, ohne ein Hilfsverb oder "to do" zu Hilfe zu nehmen.

Example:

subject	predicate	object	
Bob and Peter	like	ice-cream	Aussagesatz
Mary and Brenda	do not like	ice-cream	Verneinung

Hier ist eine weitere Besonderheit. Wie bei der umschriebenen Frage (s. Seite 84 ff.) wandert auch bei der Verneinung das "-s" des Verbs bei der dritten Person Einzahl zum "do". Es wird dann zu **"does"**

Example: Bob likes to go to school.

Verneinung: Bob does not (doesn't) like to go to school.

Das Verb hat hinter "do/does" keine Endung. Es steht dann in der Grundform.

1. Eating and drinking – Likes and dislikes

ice-cream	spinach	rolls	apples	fish	cheese
Coke	water	milk	whisky	lemonade	coffee

Setze ein:

I like ice-cream _____ but I don't like apples.

_____ but _____

_____ but _____

_____ but _____

_____ but _____

Wie wird die Verneinung gebildet?

I. Enthält der Satz, der verneint werden soll, ein **Hilfsverb** ("can – may – must – will" etc.) oder eine Form von **"to be"** ("am – are – is – was – were"), dann wird nur das Wörtchen "not" hinzugefügt.

→ Peter is short   → Peter is not short
→ Bob can speak English   → Bob cannot speak English
→ You may go out   → You may not go out

II. Enthält der Satz, der verneint werden soll, **keine** Form von "to be" und auch kein Hilfsverb, dann braucht man die Hilfe von "to do"! Dazu kommt die Verneinung "not"! Das Verb steht nach do + not in der Grundform ohne "to".

→ Cats drink milk.   → Cats do not drink coffee.
→ Peter and Father help Mother.   → Peter and Father do not help Mother.

III. Das **-s** der **3.** Person Singular wandert bei der Verneinung vom Verb an das Hilfsverb "do".

A bus-driver drives buses → A bus-driver doesn't drive tractors.
Mother shuts the window → Mother doesn't shut the door.

2. Likes/dislikes

Sieh Dir die Bilder an und schreibe auf, was Vater mag und was nicht.

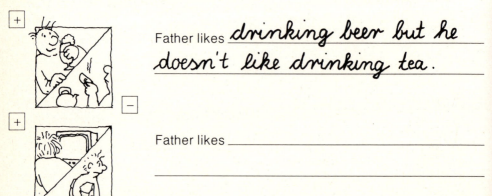

Father likes *drinking beer but he doesn't like drinking tea.*

Father likes _____

Father _____

_____

Father _____

_____

_____

_____

3. Jobs – Berufe

Fülle die Lücken aus, wie das Beispiel zeigt.

A nurse	*doesn't*	sell things.	She *helps people*.
A butcher		teach children.	He _____
A shop assistant		fly a plane.	_____
A teacher		make sausages.	_____
A pilot		clean the rooms.	_____
A pop star		help people.	_____
A charwoman		sing hits.	_____

Enthält der Satz, den Du verneinen willst, keine Form von **"to be"**, aber auch kein **Hilfsverb**, dann mußt Du "to do" zu Hilfe nehmen. Das "-s" der 3. Person Singular wandert vom Vollverb zum Hilfsverb "do" → doesn't.

4. Mixed exercise

Bilde jeweils einen Aussagesatz +, *die Verneinung* − *und die Frage* ?

television   *I watch TV.*
                 I don't watch TV.   + −
I/watch   *Do I watch TV?*   ?

cake
                                       + −
you/make   ?

ball
                                       + −
he/play   ?

book
                                       + −
she/read   ?

bone/dog
                                       + −
it/eat   ?

bike
                                       + −
we/ride   ?

tea _____

_____ _____ | + |
                                     | − |
they/drink _____ | ? |

5. Mixed exercise
(Hilfsverben und Vollverben vermischt)

Schreibe jeweils als Antwort auf diese Fragen kurze Sätze, die mit "yes" oder "no" beginnen.

1. Can a dog run? *Yes, it can.*
2. Do fish wear hats? *No, they don't.*
3. Is snow white? _____
4. Are stones good to eat? _____
5. Do monkeys read books? _____
6. Do ducks like swimming? _____
7. Can pigs drive a car? _____
8. Is six more than five? _____
9. Do tigers go to school? _____
10. Are boys allowed to drive a car? _____
11. Do carrots grow on trees? _____
12. Are oranges black? _____

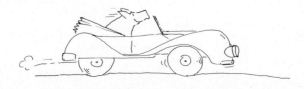

9 QUESTION WORDS

Interrogativ-Pronomen (Fragefürwörter)

Part 1   The forms

Fragefürwörter fragen nach Personen oder Sachen. Sie vertreten das Satzglied, nach dem Du fragst.

1. Formen

1. Who? → fragt nach **Personen** — wer?
[hu:]
(persons)   Es fragt nach dem Subjekt (Person/en) oder dem Objekt (Person/en)

    Who is the boy over there? → **He's** my brother Peter.
    Who do you see? → I see my **father.**

2. What? → fragt nach **Handlungen oder Sachen** — was?
[wɔt]
(things)   Es fragt nach dem Subjekt **oder** dem Objekt.

    What's that in English? → A car. (subject)
    What do you see? → I see a **child.** (object)

Wenn "who" oder "what" nach dem Subjekt fragen, wird das Verb im Fragesatz nicht mit "to do" umschrieben. Es lautet genauso wie im Aussagesatz. Wenn "who" oder "what" nach dem Objekt fragen, wird das Verb mit "do/does/did" umschrieben.

3. where? → fragt nach dem **Ort** — wo?
[weə]
(place)

    Where are you from? → From Kiel.

4. when? → fragt nach der **Zeit** — wann?
[wen]
(time)

    When do you go to London? → Next year.

2. Asking questions

Aussagesatz:	Mr. Black drinks whisky .
Fragesatz:	What does Mr. Black drink?
	Auch hier wandert das "-s" zur Form von "to do". "what" fragt hier nach dem Objekt (Sache) (Einzahl)
Aussagesatz:	We like apples.
Fragesatz:	What do we like?
	"what" fragt hier nach dem Objekt (Sache) (Mehrzahl)
Aussagesatz:	We help our mother in the household.
Fragesatz:	Who do we help in the household?
	"who" fragt hier nach dem Objekt bei Personen
Aussagesatz:	The children play in the classroom.
Fragesatz:	Where do the children play?
	"where" fragt nach der adverbialen Bestimmung des Ortes
Aussagesatz:	Father wash**es** his car every Sunday.
Fragesatz:	When do**es** father wash his car?
	"when" fragt nach der adverbialen Bestimmung der Zeit

3. Hier sehen wir uns die Sache im Satz an:

	subject who?	verb predicate	object what? who?	adverb of place where? (Ort)	adverb of time when? (Zeit)
I.	Mr. Black nach dem Subjekt fragt man mit who oder	drinks	whisky nach dem Objekt fragt man mit what oder		
II.	This magazine what? ←	shows	nice people who? ←		
III.	Mother	writes	a letter to Uncle Henry what? who?		

IV.	Mother	writes	a letter to Uncle Henry	in the kitchen nach der adverbialen Bestimmung des Ortes fragt man mit where?	
V.	Mother	writes	a letter to Uncle Henry	in the kitchen	on Sunday nach der adverbialen Bestimmung der Zeit fragt man mit when?

4. More question words

Hier sind weitere Fragefürwörter.

which? → fragt nach der **Auswahl von Personen und Sachen**
[witʃ] aus einer bestimmten Anzahl – welche(r)?
selection Which do you like better, coffee or milk?
Which of you was the first?

whose? → fragt nach dem **Besitz** – wessen?
[hu:z] Whose hat is this? Brenda's.
possession

why? → fragt nach dem **Grund** – warum?
[wai] als Antwort folgt because – weil
reason Why do you get up so late? – Because I feel ill today.

how? → fragt nach der **Art und Weise** – wie?
[hau] How are you? – Thanks, fine.
manner

how much? → fragt nach der **Menge** (Einzahl) – wieviel?
[hau mʌtʃ] How much sugar have we got?
quantity

how many? → fragt nach der **Anzahl** (Mehrzahl) – wieviel?
[hav 'mæni] How many shirts have you got?
number

5. **Test yourself**
Achtung: Hilfsverben werden nicht mit "to do" umschrieben.
Ask questions with "what" that get these answers:

1. Q.: *What does father like* _____?
   A.: Father likes beer.

2. Q.: _____?
   A.: David is doing his homework.

3. Q.: _____ against?
   A.: The bikes lean against the wall.

4. Q.: _____?
   A.: The children are playing ball.

6. *Ask questions about the underlined words.*
Frage nach den unterstrichenen Satzteilen. Schreibe die Fragen in Dein Heft.

1. They see the Alps.

   What do they see?

2. I'm going to build a garage.
3. We're planning our summer holiday.
4. The teacher knows the names of all his pupils.
5. The driver cannot stop the bus.
6. Tom feeds his goldfish on little worms.

7. *Ask questions with "where" that get these answers:*

1. Q.: *Where is Kiel* _____?
   A.: Kiel is in Germany.

2. Q.: _____?
   A.: You can get stamps at the post office.

3. Q.: _____?
   A.: You must go to the station to get a ticket.

4. Q.: _____?
   A.: Kate and Paul live at No. 6 Downing Street.

5. Q.: _____?
A.: The dogs are in the garden.

6. Q.: _____?
A.: Queen Elizabeth lives in Buckingham Palace.

7. Q.: _____?
A.: Edinburgh is in Scotland.

8. Q.: _____?
A.: Germans live in Germany.

9. Q.: _____?
A.: You can get a newspaper at a newsagent's.

8. *Ask questions with "when" that get these answers:*

1. Q.: _____?
A.: Aunt Mary arrives at 10.30.

2. Q.: _____?
A.: Christmas Eve is on the 24th Dec.

3. Q.: _____?
A.: School begins at 21st August.

4. Q.: _____?
A.: There was a lot of noise last night.

5. Q.: _____?
A.: Father and Mother get up at six o'clock.

9. ## What do you do on weekdays?

Beantworte die Fragen und nenne die Uhrzeit:

When do you get up?

_____

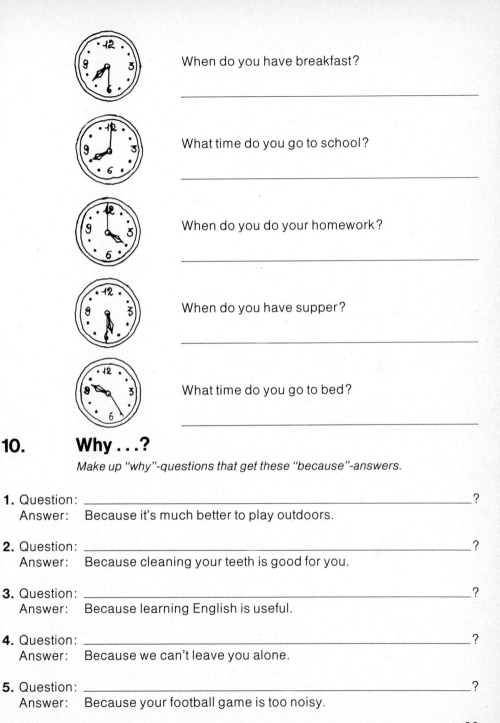

When do you have breakfast?
_____

What time do you go to school?
_____

When do you do your homework?
_____

When do you have supper?
_____

What time do you go to bed?
_____

10. Why . . . ?

Make up "why"-questions that get these "because"-answers.

1. Question: _____?
   Answer: Because it's much better to play outdoors.

2. Question: _____?
   Answer: Because cleaning your teeth is good for you.

3. Question: _____?
   Answer: Because learning English is useful.

4. Question: _____?
   Answer: Because we can't leave you alone.

5. Question: _____?
   Answer: Because your football game is too noisy.

11. Dialogue

Fill in this dialogue.
Setze "why" und "because" ein.

Son: Mummy, _____ have I got to learn English?

Mother: _____ it's good for you.

Son: But _____ have I got to learn it when I don't like it?

Mother: _____ you'll need it.
Son: But I hate it!
Mother: No, son, it's a nice language.
Son: But I like maths and physics better.
Mother: English is better.
Son: But I want to become an engineer!
Mother: English is very useful.

Son: But, Mummy, _____ have I got to learn English when it's so hard?

Mother: _____ you have to!!

12. An interview

Give the answers.
Du wirst jetzt interviewt. Beantworte die Fragen des Reporters.

Reporter: Hello, can you answer some questions?

You: *Yes,* _____ [+]
Reporter: They are about your way to school every day. My first question is: how do you get there – by bicycle, by bus, on foot, or how?

You: _____
_____ [bus]

Reporter: I see. How far is it from your home?

You: _____
_____ [10 km]

Reporter: Can you tell me how long it takes you?

You: _____

_____ [½ hr]

Reporter: Where do you live?

You: _____

_____ [Kiel]

Reporter: And where do you go to school?

You: _____

_____ [a Realschule]

Reporter: Well, thank you very much!

13. "Who?" – "What?"

Eine Besonderheit ist die Frage nach dem Subjekt Who? / What?

	S	P	O
Aussagesatz:	Fred	likes	bananas.
Fragesatz:	Who	like**s**	bananas?
	"Who" (wer) ist hier selbst Subjekt. Es braucht also nicht mit "to do" umschrieben zu werden.		
	S	P	O
Aussagesatz:	The bikes	belong	to Brenda.
Fragesatz:	What	belong**s**	to Brenda?
	"What" (was) ist hier selbst Subjekt. Es braucht also nicht mit "to do" umschrieben zu werden.		

Fragst Du nach dem Subjekt, so wird die Frage durch "who" oder "what" eingeleitet.

> **who** fragt nach Personen
> **what** fragt nach Sachen

Nach "who" und "what" hat das Vollverb in Fragesätzen immer ein "**-s**", ganz gleich, ob das Subjekt des Aussagesatzes im Singular oder Plural steht. Das Hilfsverb bleibt, wie es ist.

14. Test yourself

Ask questions with "Who" that get these answers!

1. Q.: *Who is with Brenda* ?
A.: It's her boyfriend Paul.

2. Q.: _____?
A.: Father washes the car.

3. Q.: _____?
A.: Molly has a dog.

4. Q.: _____?
A.: Peter and Paul like fish.

5. Q.: _____?
A.: John is Brenda's brother.

6. Q.: _____ can speak English?
A.: We all can.

15. Who in your family does it?

Ask the questions and give the answers.
Stelle die Fragen und gib die Antworten.

	Questions	Answers
go shopping (einkaufen)	*Who goes shopping?*	Mother *goes shopping.*
wash up (abwaschen)	_____ ?	Mother _____
wash the car (Auto waschen)	_____ ?	Father _____

earn the money
(Geld verdienen) _____ ? Mother and Father _____

make breakfast
(Frühstück machen) _____ ? My sister _____

keep the house clean
(saubermachen) _____ ? Our charwoman _____

16. A riddle

Questions with "what" ("what" fragt nach dem Subjekt):

1. What has arms but no hands? _____
2. What grows bigger the more you take away from it? _____

3. What long word has only one letter in it? _____
4. What is so fragile (zerbrechlich) that it breaks when you speak?

17. Mixed exercise

| Where? / Who? / What? / When? |

Ordne die Fragen und Antworten zu! Schreibe dann die Fragen mit den Antworten in Dein Heft.

1	Who's that?	A	It's from me.	1	B
2	What's her name?	B	My girlfriend Brenda.	2	
3	Where's she from?	C	She's from Scotland.	3	
4	Who are you?	D	Last Wednesday.	4	
5	When did you come here?	E	I'm her girlfriend.	5	
6	What are we going to do?	F	Brenda Peabody.	6	
7	Who is the ball from?	G	Let's go to the swimming pool.	7	

who und where werden leicht verwechselt!
Dieses Schema kann eine Merkhilfe sein.

| there | ← where? | who? → | you |

↓ ↓
wo? wer?

Sätze mit Hilfsverben werden natürlich nicht mit "to do" umschrieben, auch wenn ein anderes Wort davorsteht.

18. **Exercise** *Setze who/where ein.*

1. _____ is Brenda's sister? – Her sister is Mary.
2. _____ is Father now? – He's in the garden.
3. _____ is that boy over there? – That's Peter.
4. _____ is my English book? – It's on your desk.
5. _____ do you go this afternoon? – I go to the beach.
6. _____ goes over there? – He is our English teacher.
7. _____ have you put your coat? – It's in the wardrobe.
8. _____ is playing football? – Peter and Henry.

19. **Who/where/what/how?**
Setze das richtige Fragewort ein!

	Question	**Answer**
1.	_____ is your name?	Brenda.
2.	_____ old are you?	I'm twelve.
3.	_____ are the papers?	They are on the table.
4.	_____ many balls have you got?	Two.
5.	_____ is playing football?	My friends are playing.
6.	_____ time is it?	It's half past three.

7. _____ wants ice-cream?   Kitty and Sarah.

8. _____ is she sitting?   Under a tree.

9. _____ many pupils can you count? Twenty-three.

10. _____ is the dog?   It's in the box.

11. _____ much is this book?   It's 2 pounds.

12. _____ is sitting on the table? The monkey.

13. _____ have you got in your hand? A present for you.

20. Ask for the underlined parts
Frage nach den unterstrichenen Satzteilen.

1. _____
   Tom is an assistant in a shop.

2. _____
   The shop sells newspapers, pens and pencils.

3. _____
   Mrs. Sim is Mr. Dent's sister.

4. _____
   Mr. and Mrs. Brown have a small house in Wimbledon.

5. _____
   He is downstairs in the sitting room.

6. _____
   The man at the entrance looks at the tickets.

7. _____
   The film begins at 6 p.m.

8. _____
   It is the rush hour.

9. _____
   Miss Betty wants a newspaper.

Part 2 How to say it?

1. Interviewing people

Peter O'Toole stays in Germany for some weeks with his penfriend Katrin. One day he visits Katrin's class teacher at school.
The pupils ask a lot of questions. Start here

questions (Fragen)	answers (Antworten)		questions (Fragen)
	Peter O'Toole		1. What's your name?
2. Where are you from?	Great Britain	London	3. From where in GB?
4. When were you born?	11th Oct.	11 yrs	5. How old are you?
6. How many brothers and sisters have you got?	2 br	1 si	
	English	French	7. What languages do you speak?
8. What kind of house do you live in?	flat	6 rooms	9. How many rooms has your flat got?
10. What is your father's job?	Father: teacher	Mother: housewife	11. What is your mother's job?
12. What are your hobbies?	swimming collecting stamps +	doing homework helping mother −	13. What don't you like?
14. When do you go back to GB?	next week	because I want to say hallo to you	15. Why do you visit our school?
	Kiel? Super!		16. How do you like Kiel?

Schreibe jetzt die Fragen in Dein Heft und beantworte sie.

Example: *Where are you from?*
I'm from Great Britain.

10 AT THE STATION

Part 1   Vocabulary

1.   *Ordne die Wörter den Nummern zu. Schreibe in Dein Heft.*

train / engine / platform / compartment / station-clock / passengers / newsstand / locker / guard / porter / luggage / suitcase / rails / ticket-office

2. At the railway station

Fill in the words from the list.

People buy _____ for the _____. They get _____ and _____ the trains. _____ carry suitcases. _____ wait for their trains on a _____. At the _____ people buy _____.

Some people are _____. They hurry to get the train.

| platform |
| ticket-office |
| trains |
| on |
| off |
| passengers |
| porters |
| late |
| tickets |

Part 2 How to say it?

Dialogues at the station

1. Travelling by train

Translation exercise

Read the dialogues and learn them by heart.
Lies die Dialoge und lerne sie auswendig. Übersetze dann die Dialoge und schreibe sie auf!

a) Asking a railway official (Bahnbeamter)

Brenda: Can you help me, please?
Official: Yes?
Brenda: When does the next train to Birmingham leave?
Official: Wait a minute – the next train to Birmingham leaves at 14.02 (fourteen-oh-two).
Brenda: And when does it arrive?
Official: At 16.15.
Brenda: OK. And which platform does it leave from?
Official: Platform two.
Brenda: Thank you.
Official: You're welcome. (Bitte sehr.)

b) At the ticket-office

Lady: One and a half single to Brighton, please!
Clerk: Is that half for that young gentleman?
(Beamter)

Lady:	Yes, he is my son.
Clerk:	How old is he?
Lady:	He's twelve.
Clerk:	Is he? He looks a big boy for his age.
Lady:	Yes, he does.
Clerk:	One and a half to Brighton. That's 7 pounds, please.
Lady:	Thanks. Come on, Richard. We are late.

c) At the ticket-office

Gentleman:	Two tickets to London, please.
Clerk:	Single or return?
Gentleman:	How much is the single fare?
Clerk:	Four pounds.
Gentleman:	Is the return cheaper (billiger) than two singles?
Clerk:	Yes, sir.
Gentleman:	Two returns, then.
Clerk:	Right! Two returns London. Twelve pounds, please.

A little rhyme. Learn it by heart.

There was a young lady named Sue,
who wanted to catch the 2.02. [tu: tu:]
Said the porter, "Don't hurry,
don't hurry or worry:
It's a minute or two to 2.02."

2. Einen Bahnbeamten (railway official) um Auskunft bitten

Wie Du es sagen kannst	Was Du sagen willst
Can you help me, please?	Ihn ansprechen
When does the next train to ... leave? When does the next train from ... arrive?	Nach der Abfahrts-/ Ankunftszeit fragen
Which platform does it leave from? Which platform does it arrive at?	Nach dem Bahnsteig fragen

3. Am Fahrkartenschalter

A single ticket to ..., please. A return ticket to ..., please.	Eine Hin- oder Rückfahrkarte kaufen
A half single ticket to ..., please. A half return ticket to ..., please.	Eine Kinderfahrkarte kaufen
How much does it cost? How much is it? How much is a ticket to ...? What does a ticket to ... cost?	Nach dem Preis einer Fahrkarte fragen

4. Wie man sich nach der Abfahrtszeit erkundigt
Schreibe das Gespräch auf.

Mary: _____
   begrüßt den Angestellten (clerk) und fragt, wann der nächste Zug nach Ipswich abfährt.

Clerk: _____
   gibt Auskunft (11.00 Uhr).

Mary: _____
   fragt, von welchem Bahnsteig der Zug abfährt.

Clerk: _____
   sagt es ihr (Bahnsteig 4).

Mary: _____
   fragt, wann der Zug in Ipswich ist.

Clerk: _____
   zögert einen Augenblick, sagt dann die Zeit (13.00 Uhr).

Mary: _____
   bedankt sich.

11 QUESTION TAGS
Kurzfragen

Part 1 Examples/rules (Regeln)

1. Your sister is at home, <u>isn't she</u>? Deine Schwester ist doch zu Hause, nicht wahr?

2. Your parents aren't at home, <u>are they</u>? Deine Eltern sind doch nicht zu Hause, oder?

3. He'll come soon, <u>won't he</u>? Er wird doch bald kommen, nicht wahr?

Achtung: Die Verneinung von will lautet won't

4. You saw him, <u>didn't you</u>? Du sahst ihn doch, nicht wahr?

5. You don't go to the cinema, <u>do you</u>? Du gehst doch nicht ins Kino, oder?

In der Unterhaltung hängt man oft an einen Satz, der eine Behauptung ausdrückt, einen kurzen Nachsatz an, der zur Zustimmung auffordert. Im Deutschen geschieht das zumeist durch
nicht wahr? und – oder (nicht)?
Deine Schwester ist doch zu Hause, nicht wahr?
Du gehst doch nicht ins Kino, oder?
Du bist doch ein guter Schüler, nicht wahr?

Im Englischen gibt es so etwas Ähnliches, die sogenannten "question tags".
You have a cat, haven't you? –
Du hast doch eine Katze, nicht wahr?

Rule I Enthält der Satz ein Hilfsverb und ist er bejaht, wird das "question tag" mit dem Hilfsverb verneint.
You have a cat, haven't you ?
Hilfsverb + not + Pronomen (für das Subjekt).

1. Exercise

Add the "question tag" – Füge das "question tag" hinzu (Sätze mit Hilfsverben, bejaht).

Im "question tag" werden nur die verkürzten Formen gebraucht.

Bejahter Satz, Hilfsverb ⟶ Kurzform des verneinten Hilfsverbs + Pronomen

1. Your sisters are at home,   *aren't they?*
2. Jim is writing a letter,   _____ _____
3. We can play here,   _____ _____
4. It was cold yesterday,   _____ _____
5. It will be fine tomorrow,   _____ _____

Rule II Enthält der Satz ein Hilfsverb und ist er verneint, so enthält das "question tag" <u>kein</u> not.

2. Exercise

Verneinter Satz, Hilfsverb ⟶ bejahtes Hilfsverb + Pronomen

1. Helga isn't at school,   *is she?*
2. You won't go home,   _____ _____
3. They haven't heard about it,   _____ _____
4. Jim isn't eating,   _____ _____
5. Father mustn't park his car here, _____ _____

Rule III Enthält der Satz kein Hilfsverb, sondern ein Vollverb und ist er bejaht, so wird – wie bei der Frage – eine Form von "to do" – verneint – eingesetzt. Die Zeitform richtet sich nach der Zeitform des Verbs.

3. Exercise

Bejahter Satz, Vollverb	→	Kurzform des verneinten Hilfsverbs "do" + Pronomen

1.	Tom helps his father,	*doesn't he*	?
2.	You know Mr. Bluck,	_____ _____	?
3.	The bus stops here,	_____ _____	?
4.	Mother saw him,	*didn't she* (Past Tense)	?
5.	Aunt Mary went shopping,	_____ _____	?

Rule IV Ist der Hauptsatz mit einem Vollverb verneint, so enthält das "question tag" eine Form von "to do" – bejaht.

4. Exercise

Verneinter Satz, Vollverb	→	bejahtes Hilfsverb + Pronomen

1.	Peter doesn't know this story,	*does he*	?
2.	Boys don't cry,	_____ _____	?
3.	You didn't see her,	_____ _____	?
4.	We don't stop here,	_____ _____	?
5.	Father and Mother don't go out,	_____ _____	?

5. Exercise

Beende die Sätze mit "question tags".

1. He always goes to New York by plane, *doesn't he*?
2. You saw that movie, _____?
3. I paid you the money, _____?
4. His father is a rather well-known baker, _____?
5. It rains a lot in the month of April, _____?
6. Today isn't Wednesday, _____?
7. He didn't telephone you, _____?
8. They have already left for Chicago, _____?
9. Bill hasn't been here today, _____?
10. He won't be back until Wednesday, _____?
11. They have a pretty home, _____?
12. She is a lovely girl, _____?
13. You'll be in class tomorrow, _____?
14. Your watch has stopped, _____?
15. She dances very well, _____?

12 THE TENSES

Das Verb ist die einzige Wortart, die die Zeit ausdrücken kann; daher nennt man es im Deutschen auch das "Zeitwort". So ist also mit dem Verb meist eine bestimmte Zeitstufe verbunden.

Im Englischen werden die Zeiten im allgemeinen genauer beachtet als im Deutschen.

Man unterscheidet verschiedene <u>Zeitstufen</u>:

	Vergangenheit		Gegenwart	
Vorvergangenheit		Vorgegenwart		Zukunft

Part 1   Die Zeitstufen

Hier ist eine Übersicht über die Zeitstufen. Lies die drei Sätze, beginne mit: Yesterday Peter got a letter ...

(Plusquamperfekt) Vor-Vergangenheit **Past Perfect**	(Imperfekt) Vergangenheit **Past Tense**	(Perfekt) Vor-Gegenwart **Present Perfect**	(Präsens) Gegenwart **Present Tense**	(Futur) Zukunft **Present Future**
MONDAY	TUESDAY		WEDNESDAY	THURSDAY
had + 3rd form of the verb	Past Tense form of the verb -ed or irregular	has ⎱ + 3rd form have ⎰ of the verb	he she + -s it	will + infinitive of the verb
				Tomorrow Tom **will get** Peter's answer.
			Today Peter **answers** the letter	
		which he **has got** from Tom.		
	Yesterday Peter **got** a letter			
which his friend **had written** the day before.				

13 THE SIMPLE PRESENT TENSE

Die "einfache" Gegenwart wird benutzt bei Tätigkeits- und Vorgangsverben.

Wann gebraucht man das present tense?

I.	**wenn etwas wiederholt wird oder immer wieder passiert, z.B.** **often – always – usually**
	My father gets up at six every morning.
	I always play tennis on Wednesdays.
	Gewohnheiten

II.	**wenn etwas immer so ist**
	The sun rises in the east.
	The Thames flows into the North Sea.
	allgemeingültige Tatsachen

III.	**wenn Handlungen aufeinander folgen.**
	Shirley wakes up, yawns, stretches her arms, gets out of bed and goes to the bathroom.
	Erzählungen – Sportberichte – Gebrauchsanweisungen

Part 1   Das "s" in der 3. Person Einzahl

1. Englische Verben hatten ursprünglich wie im Deutschen für jede Person eine eigene Endung. Heute hat nur noch die 3. Person der Gegenwart die Endung **s**

mother
she
Peter
he
the cat
it

RUNS   to the station

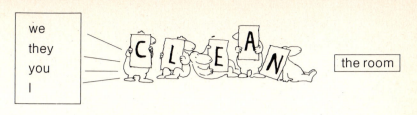

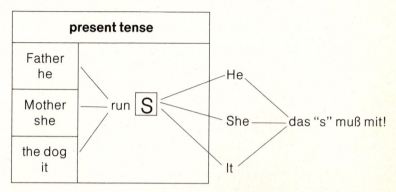

2. Wie wird das "s" geschrieben?

Schreibregeln

1. an die Grundform des Verbs wird ein "s" angehängt
   to ask – he ask**s**/to write – she write**s**
   to happen – it happen**s**

2. endet das Verb auf einen Zischlaut, so wird "es" [iz] angehängt
   to watch – he watch**es**
   to fetch – she fetch**es**
   to miss – it miss**es**

3. "y" am Ende eines Wortes wird zu "ie" wenn ein Konsonant vorausgeht
   to carry – she carr**ies**
   to fly – it fl**ies**
   to hurry – he hurr**ies**

4. "y" nach Selbstlaut bleibt "y"
   to play – she pla**ys**
   to say – he sa**ys**

Aber: I go – he go<u>es</u> [gəuz]
I do – he do<u>es</u> [dʌz]

3. ## Zu Regel 1   Exercise

Bilde die Formen der Verben in der 3. Person Einzahl.

1. She (listen) _____ to the radio every morning.

2. The bus (stop) _____ in front of the station.

3. The teacher (talk) _____ a lot every day.

4. The doctor (feel) _____ Brenda's pulse.

5. A rabbit (run) _____ not so fast as a tiger.

4. ## Zu Regel 2   Exercise 1

Lies die folgenden Verben halblaut durch und achte auf den Klang am Ende der Wörter.
Welche enden mit einem Zischlaut? Kreuze sie an.

1	×	watch	10		listen
2		go	11		brush
3		catch	12		show
4		push	13		fetch
5		carry	14		live
6		come	15		crash
7		teach	16		wash
8		kiss	17		stop
9		have	18		reach (reichen)

Exercise 2

Schreibe nun die Verben in der 3. Person Einzahl.

1. I push the door. He _____ the door.

2. You kiss your father. She _____ her father.

3. The policemen catch the thief. He _____ the thief.

4. They watch television. She _____ television.

5. The keepers fetch a bucket of water. He _____ a bucket of water. (bucket = Eimer)

5. Zu Regel 3 und 4 Exercise

y → ies nach Mitlaut
y → ys nach Selbstlaut

Ob die Endung -ies oder -ys heißt, hängt immer vom vorletzten Buchstaben ab. Ist der vorletzte Buchstabe ein Mitlaut, so wird aus y → ies: study – studies.
Ist der vorletzte Buchstabe ein Selbstlaut, so lautet die Endung -ys.

Hier sind einige Verben, deren Endung in der 3. Person Einzahl zu -ies oder -ys wird. Bilde die Formen in der 3. Person Einzahl.

try – *tries*	say – *says*
play –	enjoy –
study –	marry –
carry –	lay –
stay –	cry –
buy –	fly –
hurry –	

6. Zur Besonderheit to do/to go

Die Verben go/do haben eine Besonderheit – obwohl sie am Ende einen Selbstlaut – o – haben, wird in der 3. Person Einzahl ein -es angehängt.
Das kanntest Du bis jetzt nur bei den Zischlauten, nicht wahr?

Exercise: *Lies die Sätze laut und setze die entsprechenden Formen ein von do/go.*

1. Father _____ to the football field every weekend.

2. Peter _____ his homework after school.

3. Father and mother _____ to the cinema every Saturday.

4. I _____ to Yugoslavia in summer.

5. She _____ a test at school.

6. He _____ the washing-up when mother is not at home.

Achtung Ausspache: does = [dʌz]   goes = [gəuz]

7. The 3rd person verb machine

Die Maschine verwandelt die Verben in die 3. Person Singular. Setze die entsprechenden Formen ein.

1. You say — *he / she says*
2. they fly — _____
3. we get — _____
4. I fetch — _____
5. you do — _____
6. I buy — _____
7. they catch — _____
8. we cook — _____
9. you hurry — _____
10. I go — _____
11. you kiss — _____

8. Wie wird das "s" gesprochen?
Aussprachregeln

> 1. stimmhaft [z] nach stimmhaften Konsonanten, nach Vokalen und Diphthongen
>   to play – she plays / to drive – he drives
>   to rub – it rubs
>
> 2. stimmlos [s] nach stimmlosen Konsonanten
>   to put – he puts / to take – she takes
>   to write – it writes
>
> 3. [iz] nach Zischlauten
>   to freeze – it freezes / to watch – he watch**es**
>   to miss – she miss**es**

Verb-Endung			Aussprache	Beispiele
voiceless consonants: stimmlose Konsonanten	[k] [t] [p]	+ s	[s]	works – likes puts – wants helps – stops
voiced consonants: stimmhafte Konsonanten:	[d] [m] [n] [v]	+ s	[z]	rides – reads swims – dreams cleans – wins drives – lives
Zischlaute:	[tʃ] [s]	+ **es**	[is]	teaches – searches watches – stretches misses – kisses
vowels and diphthongs: Vokale und Diphthonge:	[ʌ] [iː] [e] [ai] [əu]	+ s	[z]	does sees hurries says flies goes

9. *Read the verbs and put them into the correct boxes!*

she
he
it

teaches – works – asks – turns right – drives – brings – makes – fetches – watches – looks – goes – sees – says – gets up – helps – takes – misses – sleeps – stops – likes – puts – tells –

[s]	[z]	[iz]
works	*brings*	*watches*

10. On holiday

Brother is on holiday. Two ways to spend a day.
Zwei Möglichkeiten, den Tag zu verbringen.   *Fill in.*

I get up at 6 o'clock.	He _____ at 11.30.
I wash and dress at once.	He never _____ and _____ before tea in the afternoon.
I go to school after breakfast.	He _____ back to bed after breakfast.
I try to get a good mark at school.	He _____ to go to sleep again.
I buy food in the supermarket.	He _____ cigarettes at the kiosk.
I help mother in the household.	He _____ himself to another bottle of beer.
I do the gardening.	He _____ his best to open a bottle of wine.
I hurry to prepare the supper.	He _____ to get into the living-room.
I watch TV in the evening.	He _____ TV in the evening, too.

11. -s or no -s ???

A normal schoolday! *Fill in the correct forms of the verbs!*

"We hate these working days", Susan and Peter

always _____.   to say

They _____ at 6.30 every morning.   to get up

Susan _____ to school at 7 o'clock.   to go

122

Peter _____ to school on his bike at 7.30.	to ride
They _____ the same lessons every day.	to have
When they _____ home Susan _____ the dinner and Peter _____ her.	to get/cook to help
After that they _____ the housework.	to do
When Father and Mother _____ from work Peter _____ upstairs and _____ his homework.	to arrive to go/do
Susan _____ down in the sitting-room and _____ some needlework.	to sit to do
After supper the whole family _____ TV.	to watch

12. *Write the correct forms of the verbs:*

1. They _____ many letters.	to write
2. Susan _____ to school with Peter every day.	to walk
3. Helen _____ to the hairdresser's very often.	to go
4. I _____ to learn English.	to want
5. Mrs. Hull _____ English.	to teach
6. We _____ in the supermarket every day.	to eat
7. David _____ this exercise very well.	to do
8. I seldom _____ to the cinema.	to go
9. I always _____ to come to school on time.	to try
10. Henry also _____ to school on foot.	to come

Part 2 Usage of the present tense

1. Gebrauch der einfachen Gegenwart
(Siehe S. 116).
Man gebraucht das "simple present tense" erstens, wenn etwas wiederholt wird oder ständig geschieht. Hierfür kannst Du die folgenden "signal words" benutzen.

often	– oft	every day	– jeden Tag
always	– immer	never	– niemals
sometimes	– manchmal	usually	– gewöhnlich
seldom	– selten	**simple present tense!**	

2. What Fred does every day in Germany
Fred ist zu Besuch in Deutschland. Das tut er jeden Tag während seines Aufenthaltes. Fülle aus:

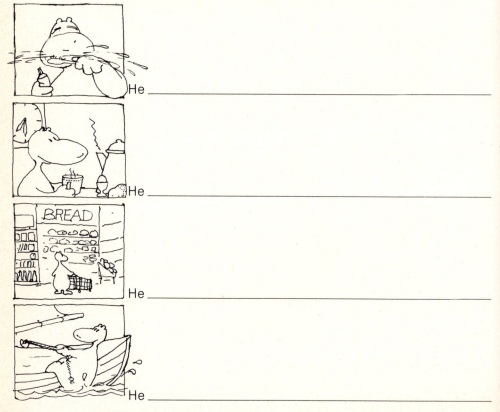

He _____

He _____

He _____

He _____

He _____

He _____

3. Saturday morning at the Carters

Put in the forms of the verbs and write the time in words.
Setze die Gegenwartsformen der Verben ein und schreibe die Zeit aus.

Mrs. Carter (to get up) _____ at _____.

Mr. Carter at _____.

At _____ Mr. and Mrs. Carter (to have) _____ breakfast.

After breakfast Mr. Carter (to read) _____ the newspaper.

Mrs. Carter (to call) _____ the children.

Susan (to get up) _____ at once, but Tom is a sleepyhead (Schlafmütze).

He (to lie) _____ in bed until _____.

At _____ Mrs. Carter (to go) _____ to the kitchen

and (to make) _____ the breakfast for the children.

At _____ Susan and Tom (to carry)

_____ the breakfast things to the kitchen.

Mrs. Carter (to wash) _____ the cups, and Betty (to help) _____ her mother.

At _____ they (to go) _____ upstairs to put on their coats,

and then they (to go) __ shopping.

Mr. Carter and Tom (to fetch) _____ water from the kitchen and (to wash) _____ the car.

At _____ they all (to sit down) _____ to lunch in the living-room.

4. A week at the Barton's

The Bartons have two children, Francis and James. Here is a plan of what each member of the family does every week.
Das spielt sich jede Woche so bei den Bartons ab.

	Mum (Mother)	Dad (Father)	Francis (daughter)	James (son)
Mon	do the washing-up, make the beds		do the shopping	water the flowers, take the dog for a walk
Tue	do the washing-up, do the shopping	make the beds		water the flowers, take the dog for a walk
Wed	do the shopping		make the beds	water the flowers, take the dog for a walk
Thur	do the washing-up, do the shopping	make the beds		water the flowers, take the dog for a walk
Fri	do the shopping		make breakfast	water the flowers, take the dog for a walk
Sat	do the washing-up	do the washing-up, make the beds	make breakfast	water the flowers, take the dog for a walk
Sun	do the washing-up		make the beds	water the flowers

Beschreibe in Deinem Heft, was die Familienmitglieder jede Woche tun: Gebrauche dabei:

often	always	sometimes	never
oft	immer	manchmal	niemals

Example:

James always water**s** the flowers and he often take**s** the dog for a walk but he never do**es** the shopping.

Mum _____

_____

Dad _____

_____

Francis _____

_____

127

Part 3 Present tense bei allgemeingültigen Tatsachen

Man gebraucht das "simple present tense" **zweitens,** wenn man sagen will, daß etwas **immer** so ist, man also eine allgemeingültige Tatsache mitteilen will.

1. What do you know about the sun?
Fill in!

It _____ in the _____. (to rise)

It _____ in the _____. (to set)

2. What do you know about the earth and the moon?

The moon _____ round the _____. (to go)

The earth _____ round the _____. (to go)

3. Describing people
What can you say about this gentleman?
Fülle den Lückentext aus, die folgenden Angaben helfen Dir dabei:

name	David	30	to be 30 years old
to live in	London	GB	to come from
to live in	flat	6 rooms	to have 6 rooms
to work as a	teacher	big school	to work in a
to speak	English	German	to speak
to be	married	4 children	to have
to like	football	Italy	
	fishing	boxing	
		TV	to hate
to play	tennis	beer	
		warm milk	
to collect	stamps		
	records		

His name is _____. He is _____.

David _____ in _____. He _____ from _____.

His home is _____. It _____ rooms. He _____ as a _____ in

a _____. David _____ English and _____.

He is _____ and has 4 _____. David likes _____ and

_____.

He plays _____. He also _____ stamps and _____.

But he _____ Italy, _____, TV, _____, and warm _____.

4.

	Katrin	Mustafa	Sven	José
to live	Regensburg	Hamburg	Copenhagen	Madrid
to come from	Germany	Turkey	Denmark	Spain
to speak	German English	Turkish German English	Danish good German	Spanish a little German
to play	table tennis	football	volley-ball	basket-ball
to collect	dolls	Turkish records	stamps	posters
to like	sweets	dancing	swimming	riding
to hate	doing homework	going to school	brown bread	spinach

Beschreibe die vier Kinder und gebrauche dabei die 3. Person Einzahl der angegebenen Verben. Schreibe in Dein Heft.
Example: Katrin <u>lives</u> in Regensburg. She <u>comes</u> from Germany and <u>speaks</u> English and German. She <u>plays</u> table tennis and <u>collects</u> dolls. She <u>likes</u> sweets and <u>hates</u> doing homework.

Part 4   Jobs – Berufe

1.   Vocabulary

Lerne die Bezeichnungen der Berufe auswendig

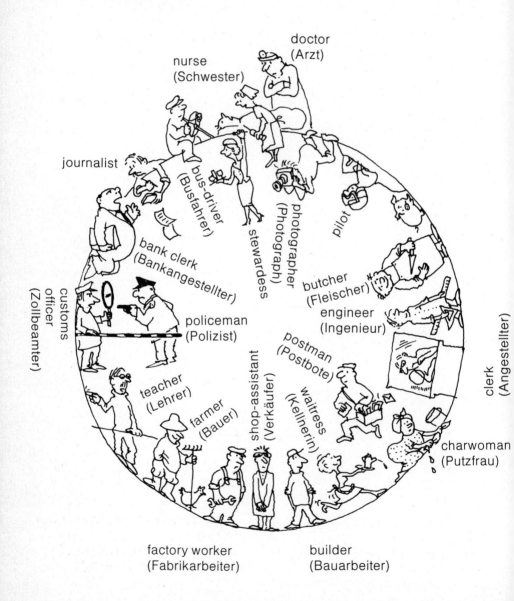

2. What am I?

Was bin ich? Schreibe die Berufe!

1. I'm a woman. I work at home. *I'm a housewife.*

2. I help sick people. _____

3. I have pupils. _____

4. I stop thieves. _____

5. I say "Three coffees, madam?" _____

6. I say "This patient is sleeping!" _____

7. I say "Shall I give you banknotes or coins, Sir?" _____

8. I bring the letters. _____

9. I clean the rooms. _____

10. I sell meat and sausages. _____

3. Do you know the jobs?

Fill in the names!

a _____

a _____

a _____

a _____

a _____

a _____

a _____

a _____

a _____   a _____   a _____

4. Matching exercise
Ordne die Hälften zu.

A	nurse	9
B	waitress	
C	teacher	
D	customs officer	
E	photographer	
F	pilot	
G	bank clerk	
H	doctor	
I	bus-driver	
J	policeman	
K	butcher	
L	charwoman	
M	farmer	
N	stewardess	
O	engineer	
P	shop-assistant	
Q	builder	
R	journalist	
S	factory worker	
T	postman	

1	to take snapshots/to develop films
2	to fly a plane/to check the controls
3	to bring letters and parcels
4	to write reports in newspapers
5	to repair machines
6	to milk cows/to drive a tractor
7	to make sausages/to sell meat
8	to help sick people/to make a diagnosis
9	to take a temperature/to wash the patients
10	to sell things in shops
11	to work in a factory
12	to help people on a plane
13	to correct test-papers/to talk a lot
14	to take orders/to serve meals
15	to build houses/to lay the bricks
16	to look for drugs/to search luggage
17	to clean the rooms
18	to drive a bus
19	to arrest criminals
20	to count money

Schreibe jetzt die Tätigkeiten der Berufe in Dein Heft.

Achtung! Wenn man über Berufe spricht, gebraucht man meist das "simple present tense", weil man eine allgemeingültige Tatsache mitteilt.

Example:
A) She takes a temperature and washes the patients. She works as a nurse.

5. Reading comprehension (Leseverstehen)
A terrible story about jobs.
This story is in the "past tense".

Vater erinnert sich ... Lies die Geschichte.

When I was a student I was very poor so I had to do part-time jobs (Gelegenheitsarbeiten) in my holidays. One year I worked as a postman, the second year I worked as a mechanic in a garage and the third year I was a school assistant in a big school. But in the fourth year I could not get a job. So I had to work in a butcher's shop in the day and in the evening I worked in a hospital. One evening when I went into the waiting-room in my white coat an old lady looked at me, opened her mouth and cried:

"My God, it's my butcher!"

Lies die Geschichte ein zweites Mal, decke sie dann ab und schreibe sie in Dein Heft.

Part 5 *Present tense – Handlungsfolgen*

Man gebraucht das "simple present tense" **drittens,** wenn man schildert, daß bestimmte Handlungen aufeinander folgen. Als Signalwörter werden dann meist "then – after – at last" gebraucht.

1. Getting up in the morning
What does Fred do every morning?

At six o'clock the alarm-clock (ring)
At six o'clock the alarm-clock rings.

Fred (stretch) his
Fred stretches his arms.

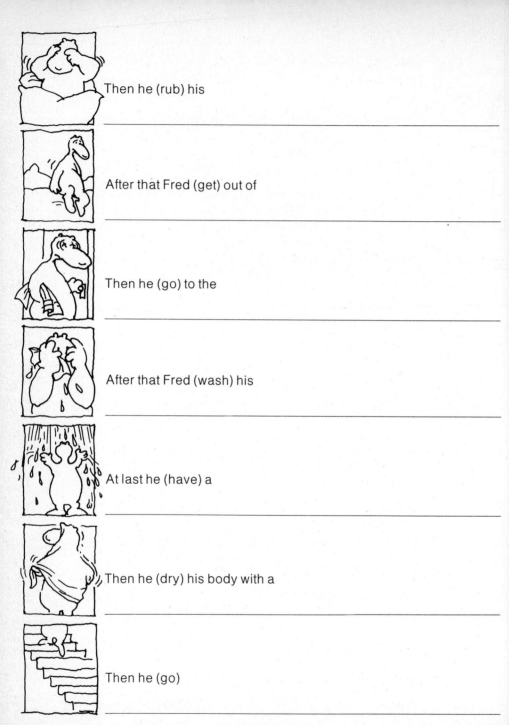

Then he (rub) his

After that Fred (get) out of

Then he (go) to the

After that Fred (wash) his

At last he (have) a

Then he (dry) his body with a

Then he (go)

and (sit) at the breakfast table and (have) breakfast

_____

_____

At 8 o'clock Fred (leave) for school

_____

2. Waking up in the morning

Schreibe auf, was auf dem Bild nach und nach passiert; Handlungsfolgen werden im "simple present tense" beschrieben.

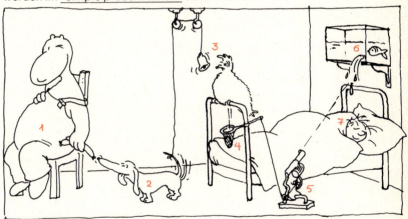

This list will help you: 1) offer sausage 2) wag tail (wackelt mit Schwanz) 3) bell ring 4) hen lay an egg; egg fall into net 5) revolver fire 6) water fall 7) sleeping boy wake up

Gebrauche auch die Signalwörter "first – then – after – that – at last".

Example: First Fred offers a sausage to his dog.

The dog wags its _____

Then the bell _____

The hen _____

14 THE CONTINUOUS FORM

Part 1 Forms and usage – die Formen und der Gebrauch

1. The *-ing*-form (progressive form – continuous form)

Die Verlaufsform

Neben dem einfachen Präsens (simple present – siehe S. 116 ff.) gibt es im Englischen noch die sogenannte "continuous form" oder "progressive form".

Die einfache Gegenwart wird – wie Du natürlich schon weißt – angewandt, wenn allgemeine Tatsachen oder immer wiederkehrende Handlungen ausgedrückt werden sollen.

The house **stands** by the road.	Das Haus steht immer dort.
Every day Mrs. Miller **prepares** the breakfast.	Jeden Tag macht Frau Miller das Frühstück.

Die Verlaufsform dagegen wird gebraucht, wenn eine Handlung von nur vorübergehender Dauer im Augenblick des Sprechens gerade vor sich geht.

Look, the milkman **is coming**.	da kommt er gerade
It **is raining**.	es regnet gerade
The dog **is barking**.	der Hund bellt gerade

Du siehst, Wörter wie "gerade, im Augenblick" usw. werden im Englischen nicht übersetzt. Man nimmt dafür die "continuous form". Die Verlaufsform wird aus **den Formen des Hilfszeitwortes "to be"** (siehe S. 27 ff.) und dem **Mittelwort der Gegenwart** gebildet (present participle). Dies erhält man, indem man die Silbe **"-ing"** an die Grundform der Verben (ohne to) anhängt.

You see

action ⟷ we use
at the moment   the progressive form

The progressive form has two parts:
(in der Gegenwart)

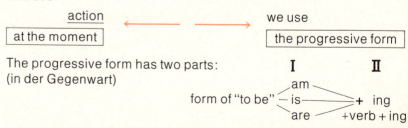

2. Exercise

Fill in the forms of "to be" and the present participle of the verb.
Setze die Formen von "to be" und das Partizip Präsens ein.

	person	simple present (always)	progressive form (now)
SINGULAR	1st	I work	I am working
	2nd	you work	you _____ working
	3rd	he works	he _____ work _____
		she works	she _____ work _____
		it works	it _____ work _____
PLURAL	1st	we work	we _____ work _____
	2nd	you work	you _____ work _____
	3rd	they work	they _____ work _____

3. Die Schreibung der *-ing*-Form

Bei den meisten Verben kannst Du einfach eine Form von "to be" bilden und an die Grundform des Verbs die Silbe "ing" anhängen, um die "progressive form" zu erhalten.
Bei einigen Verben ist das aber etwas anders.
Sieh selbst!

Father is smoking a cigar. Grundform des Verbs: to smok**e**
Mother is closing the window. Grundform des Verbs: to clos**e**

Was ist passiert?
Das stumme "**e**" am Ende der Verben ist verschwunden.

| smoke + ing = smoking | | close + ing = closing |

Merke: Wenn ein Verb am Schluß ein "e" hat, so geht dieses "e" bei der "*-ing*-Form" verloren.

Ein englischer Reim sagt hierüber:
"When adding -ING
the E takes wing." (Flügel)
(verschwindet das "e")

4. The Evans are in the sitting-room, Mother is working in the kitchen. What are the Evans doing?
Fill in.

1. Brenda _____ her boyfriend. (to telephone)

2. Father _____ a cigar in his armchair. (to smoke)

3. Peter _____ a letter to his teacher. (to write)

4. Mother _____ supper in the kitchen. (to prepare)

5. Hier ist noch eine andere Gruppe von Verben, die eine Besonderheit aufweisen, wenn man die "*-ing*-Form" bildet.

	Grundform
The butcher is cutting the meat	→ to cut
Father is sitting in an armchair	→ to sit

Was ist passiert?
Der Mitlaut nach kurzem, betontem Selbstlaut wird verdoppelt.

6. Exercise

What are the Evans doing? Fill in.

1. Mother _____ bread. (to cut)

2. Peter _____. (to get up)

3. Brenda _____ in the water. (to swim)

4. Father _____ the window. (to close)

5. Fred _____ after the ball. (to run)

6. Fred _____ the first prize. (to win)

7. Mixed exercise

Fill in the forms of "to be" and the "-ing-forms" of the verbs.

Person	to **be**	**-ing**-form	Verb
I	am	playing	to play
you			to run
he			to smile
she			to give
it			to have
Father			to sit
Mother			to cry
we			to win
you and me			to get up
you			to write
they			to dance

8. Present continuous tense

Hier sind einige Sätze in der Verlaufsform der Gegenwart. Schreibe die richtigen Formen in die Lücken.

1. She __is waiting__ (to wait) for me on the corner now.

2. Look! It _____ (to begin) to rain.

3. The train _____ (to leave) at this moment.

4. Peter _____ (to do) his homework now.

5. They _____ (to take) a walk along Elm Street.

6. I _____ (to begin) to understand English now.

7. Listen! Someone _____ (to knock) at the door.

8. The bus _____ (to stop) for us now.

9. All the children _____ (to play) in the garden now.

10. Mother _____ (to prepare) the breakfast.

9. Wiederholung der Regeln

1. Wie bildet man die "continuous form" der Gegenwart?
   Indem man eine Form von "to be" bildet und an das Verb einfach "**-ing**" anhängt.

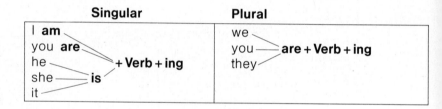

2. Wie bildet man die "**-ing**-Form" des Verbs?

   a) indem man einfach die Silbe -ing anhängt;

go + ing → going

   b) bei Verben mit kurzem Vokal wird der Mitlaut vor dem **-ing** verdoppelt.

cut	→ cu**tt**ing
stop	→ sto**pp**ing
swim	→ swi**mm**ing

   c) Wenn ein Verb am Schluß ein -e hat, geht dieses verloren.

take	→ ta**k**ing
come	→ co**m**ing

Part 2 Simple form – continuous form

Die "continuous form" drückt aus, daß eine Handlung gerade vor sich geht. Besonders häufig ist sie daher, wenn ein Wort im Satz darauf hinweist, daß die Handlung gerade abläuft.
Solche Hinweiswörter (signal words) sind "listen – horch", "look – schau" und "just – gerade".
Die "continuous form" darf nicht stehen, wenn die Handlung wiederholt erscheint oder zwei Handlungen hintereinander ablaufen (siehe S. 116).

1. Exercise

Setze jeweils die richtige Verbform in die Lücken ein. Überlege dabei jedesmal, ob sich die Handlung gerade im Augenblick abspielt,
Signal words: now – just – at this moment – listen – look,
oder ob die Handlung wiederholt – immer – oder aufeinanderfolgend geschieht.
Signal words: always – ever – never – sometimes – seldom – etc.

1. He _____ (write) many letters to his friends.

2. Look! It _____ (begin) to rain.

3. We _____ (have) our English lesson now.

4. Mr. Evans _____ (smoke) very much.

5. The bus always _____ (stop) at this corner.

6. Listen! Someone _____ (knock) at the door.

7. We _____ (have) English lessons four times a week.

8. Father is busy now. He _____ (write) a letter.

9. I always _____ (get) on the bus at this corner.

10. The bell _____ (ring) now.

141

2. A lazy holiday

Mr. Evans is on holiday. It's the first day of his holidays.
Fill in the forms of the verb.

On workdays Mr. Evans _____ (get up) at 6.00.
But today is his holiday and he can sleep longer. Usually he can't lie in bed as long as he likes. But now it's 9.00 and

he _____ (still lie) in bed.

Usually he has breakfast in a hurry. But now he _____

_____ (sit) at the breakfast table and _____ (read) the paper.

Every day he _____ (drive) into the city.

But now he _____ (drive) into the country.

Usually he _____ (run) up the stairs to his office.

But now he _____ (run) about with his dog.

Usually he _____ (sit) in his office the whole day.

But now he _____ (sit) on the beach.

3. Continuous form or simple form? – Achte auf die "signal words".

1. Look, Tom *is sitting* at his desk.	to sit
2. He _____ a letter.	to write
3. His German pen friend _____ often.	to write
4. Listen, the children _____ from 1 to ten.	to count
5. Every morning I _____ at 6 o'clock.	to get up
6. Sometimes I _____ in bed a little longer.	to lie

7. My husband _____ his newspaper. | to read
8. Look, there he _____ in an armchair. | to sit
9. The Bartons _____ tea every afternoon. | to drink
10. Look, today they _____ tea in the garden. | to have
11. Listen, Tom's dog _____. | to bark
12. Every morning the dog _____ to the bus with Tom. | to hurry
13. Look, there they _____ after a big red ball. | to run
14. Every Friday Tom _____ to bed late. | to go
15. On Saturday afternoon he and his friends _____ games in the garden. | to play
16. He _____ no lessons on Saturday. | to have

4. **Mrs. Schröter is absent**

Dies schreibt Brenda – ein englisches Mädchen aus Croydon – über einen Tag, den sie an einer deutschen Schule verbringt.
Setze die richtigen Formen der Verben in die Lücken ein.
Überlege, ob es die "continuous form" oder das "simple present tense" sein muß.

On Monday we usually (have) _____ 6 lessons. The fourth lesson is English. Mrs. Schröter, the English teacher, usually (come) _____ into the classroom at 11.30. But today she isn't at school, and so we (have) _____ a nice time. Two boys (play) _____ football with a coke bottle. They usually (use) _____ the duster but at the moment Ute (clean) _____ the board with it. Stephan (sit) _____ under the desk. He (read) _____ Mickey Mouse. He always (read) _____ comics in the classroom. Carsten (draw) _____ a funny picture on the board. It's a picture of Mr. Ziermann. Mr. Ziermann (teach) _____ mathematics at this school. Stephanie and André (write) _____ their names on the window-pane with a felt pen. They (love) _____ each other very much. Many of the girls (do) _____ their homework now. Some of the boys (look) _____ out of the window. They (watch) _____ other pupils playing football. At this moment Mr. Ziermann (come) _____ into the classroom. He is very angry about the noise in the classroom.

15 THE PAST TENSE

Part 1   Signal words/past tense

1.   Das "past tense" (die einfache Vergangenheit) gibt an,
   a) daß ein Vorgang in der Vergangenheit völlig abgeschlossen wurde; es steht dann entweder in Verbindung mit einer Zeitbestimmung der Vergangenheit oder einer Ortsangabe.
   Signalwörter, die anzeigen, daß Du das "past tense" verwenden mußt:

> yesterday, last night, in 1970, last month, last week, last year, ago (vor), long ago, an hour ago, at Christmas, once (einst), the other day (neulich), during the winter.

   b) Das Past tense steht auch, wenn der Sinnzusammenhang eindeutig auf die Vergangenheit hinweist.

2.   Hier sind noch einmal die "signal words" der beiden Zeiten "present" und "past tense" gegenübergestellt.

past	←——→	present
yesterday		this moment
last night		this hour
last month		this morning
last week		today
last year		this month
an hour ago		this year
in 1970		in this century (Jahrhundert)
the other day		
during the winter		

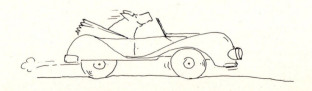

Part 2   The verb in the past – regular – (Das Zeitwort in der Vergangenheit – regelmäßig –)

1. Es gibt zwei Arten von Zeitwörtern; die einen bilden ihre Vergangenheit unregelmäßig (siehe S. 150 ff.), die anderen regelmäßig. Die regelmäßige Vergangenheit wird gebildet, indem man an die Grundform des Zeitwortes die Endung **-ed** anhängt. Die so entstandene Form ist für alle Personen gleich – die 3. Person Einzahl hat also kein -s.

2. ### What I, you, he, she, it, we, you, they did yesterday

Yesterday		
	I	play**ed** football in the garden.
	you	wash**ed** your bicycle.
	he	paint**ed** a pretty picture.
	she	visit**ed** her aunt.
	it	bark**ed** the whole night.
	we	tri**ed** to fly a kite (Drachen).
	you	call**ed** your friend.
	they	repair**ed** the TV-set.

3. ### Die Schreibung des -ed – past tense

In der Schrift sind folgende Abweichungen zu beachten.

Example:

→ 1. Stummes End **-e** fällt weg   : to manage   – I manag**ed**
→ 2. y nach Mitlaut wird zu i   : to try   – he tri**ed**
→ 3. y nach Selbstlaut bleibt   : to play   – she play**ed**
→ 4. Endkonsonanten nach einfachem, kurzem und betontem Vokal -a/e/o/u- werden verdoppelt   : I stop   – they stopp**ed**
                                             I travel   – you travell**ed**

4. Exercise

Write the past tense form of each of these regular verbs in the blanks at the right. Schreibe die Vergangenheitsform der Verben auf die Leerzeilen.

1.	study	→ *studied*	2.	use	→	_____
3.	carry	→ _____	4.	plan	→	_____
5.	cry	→ _____	6.	enjoy	→	_____
7.	help	→ _____	8.	play	→	_____
9.	hope	→ _____	10.	marry	→	_____
11.	talk	→ _____	12.	stop	→	_____
13.	point	→ _____	14.	smoke	→	_____

5.

Change the verb of each sentence to past time and write it in the blanks at the right.
Verwandle das Verb eines jeden Satzes in die Vergangenheit und schreibe die Form auf die Leerzeilen der rechten Seite.

present tense   **past tense**

1. He arrives at school on time every day.   *arrived*

2. We walk through the park every morning.

3. I use my new biro every day.

4. Ted talks to his father after dinner.

5. We finish our lessons at one o'clock.

6. She listens to the radio every night.

7. They live in Kiel.

8. My father and my mother play volley-ball once a week.

9. My brother plans a tour round the world.

10. The dog follows the boy everywhere.

6. Das Sprechen der Endung -ed

Die Regeln lauten kurzgefaßt:

Die Endung **-ed** wird ausgesprochen:

— 1 → stimmhaft [d] nach stimmhaften Lauten (außer d).
    Stimmhafte Laute sind
    1. alle Vokale (Selbstlaute),
    2. die Konsonanten (Mitlaute) b/g/v/z/l/m/n/

— 2 → stimmlos [t] nach stimmlosen Lauten (außer t).
    Stimmlose Laute sind p/k/c/f/s/

— 3 → silbisch [id] nach den Zahnlauten d + t.

7. Here are the forms

Lies die Sätze laut vor!

I looked [d]	Rule I	[lukt]
you showed down [d]	Rule I	[ʃəud]
he passed the house [t]	Rule II	[pɑːst]
she kicked the ball [t]	Rule II	[kikt]
it barked the whole day [t]	Rule II	[bɑːkt]
we watched TV every Sunday [t]	Rule II	[wɔtʃt]
you wanted to buy bread [id]	Rule III	[wɔntid]
they landed in London [id]	Rule III	[lændid]

8. Pronunciation (Aussprache)

Pronounce the following past tense forms.
Lies die folgenden Formen des Verbs in der Vergangenheit laut und schreibe die Lautung der Endung -ed in die Lücken.

[d] – [t] – [id]

1. ended [id]
2. smoked [___]
3. asked [___]
4. lived [___]
5. pulled [___]
6. painted [___]
7. picked [___]
8. showed [___]
9. worked [___]

10. washed [____]   11. waited [____]   12. stopped [____]

13. looked [____]   14. closed [____]   15. changed [____]

16. used [____]   17. pulled [____]   18. landed [____]

19. crossed [____]   20. boiled [____]   21. touched [____]

Part 3 The verb in the past (irregular)

1. Die Vergangenheit von unregelmäßigen Verben

Manche Verben haben im Englischen in der <u>Vergangenheit</u> und dem <u>Mittelwort der Vergangenheit</u> eine besondere Form. Diese drei Formen – die sogenannten Stammformen – <u>mußt Du einfach lernen</u>. Du kannst sie nicht nach einer Regel (zum Beispiel: das Past wird mit der Endung -ed gebildet) bilden. Diese Verben heißen deshalb auch unregelmäßig (irregular).

1. Die erste Stammform bezeichnet den "infinitive" (Grundform/Nennform/Infinitiv).
2. Die zweite Stammform bezeichnet das "past" (Vergangenheit).
3. Die dritte Stammform bezeichnet das "past participle" (Mittelwort der Vergangenheit, Partizip Perfekt).

2. Irregular verbs

Teste Dein Können an der folgenden Übung.
Fill in the missing forms.

	infinitive	past	past participle	German
1.	to become	became	become	werden
2.			bought	

3.				schneiden
4.	to fight			
5.				brechen
6.		went		
7.	to leave			
8.		wore		
9.		tried		
10.			behaved	
11.				brennen
12.		took		

3. Change to the past tense

Write the past tense of the verb in the blanks at the right.
Schreibe die Vergangenheitsformen der Verben rechts auf die Linien.

1. He buys many books.   *bought*

2. She writes many letters.   _____

3. The teacher puts his books on the table.   _____

4. Mother gets up at 6 o'clock every morning.   _____

5. They have a new car.   _____

6. My brother speaks English well.   _____

7. John and father always drink beer.   _____

8. The children come to school by bus.   _____

9. Peter sits in this seat.

10. My sister drinks milk with her meals.

4. One of those days (Leseverstehen)

Mr. Evans <u>worked</u> in an office in the city. Every day he <u>got</u> up at seven o'clock, <u>made</u> his breakfast, and then went to his office by bus. He had lunch in town and came home by bus each evening.
One morning last week he woke up at nine o'clock. What a shock! He had overslept and had not heard the alarm clock. He jumped out of bed and went to the bathroom. While he was shaving he cut himself and dropped the bottle of after-shave in the bath, where it broke. At last he was ready and he rushed to the kitchen and made a cup of coffee and a sandwich. But there was no time to wait. Mr. Evans left the cup of coffee on the table, put his hat on and ran out of the house and along the road to the bus stop. A moment later a bus came and stopped. Mr. Evans got on and sat down. When he came to his office the doors were shut and there was no one there. Mr. Evans was very astonished. Had everyone overslept? But then Mr. Evans remembered (erinnerte sich). It was not a workday, it was <u>Sunday.</u>

Exercise 1
Lies die Geschichte sorgfältig und unterstreiche die Verbformen in der Vergangenheit (past tense) wie im Beispiel.

Exercise 2
Ordne die Verbformen jetzt nach regelmäßigen und unregelmäßigen Verben und Hilfsverben und trage sie in die Kästen ein.

Verbs

regular verbs	irregular verbs	auxiliary verbs (Hilfsverben)
worked	*got*	*had*

Part 4   Questions in the past tense

1. Auf den Seiten 82ff. hast Du gelernt, daß die Frage in der Gegenwart (present tense) mit **do/does + Subjekt + Grundform des Zeitworts** gebildet wird. Bei Hilfsverben wird das Hilfsverb einfach vor das Subjekt gestellt. Das gilt ebenso für die Frage in der Vergangenheit, allerdings mit dem Unterschied, daß das Hilfsverb "do/does" in der Vergangenheit zu der Vergangenheitsform "did" wird. Daraus ergibt sich also das Schema **did + Subjekt + Grundform des Zeitworts** – für alle Personen gleich.

	Subjekt	Infinitiv des Verbs	
Did	I you he/she/it we you they	a r r i v e	yesterday?

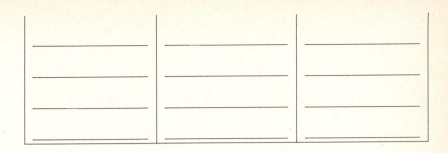

2. Bei Sätzen mit Hilfsverben – was – were – had – could – in der Vergangenheitsform werden die Hilfsverben einfach vor das Subjekt gestellt: He was in Berlin in 1980. – Was he in Berlin in 1980?

3. ## Questions with "when" in the past tense

Mr. Evans reports a burglary (Einbruch) in his office.

1. I got up at 6.50.
2. I had breakfast at 7.20.
3. I left the house at 7.45.
4. I got on the bus at 8.05.
5. I got off the bus at 8.45.
6. I entered the building at 9.35.
7. I opened the office door at 9.45.
8. I found the open safe at 9.50.
9. I phoned the police at 9.55.
10. The police came at 10.15.

*Now ask Mr. Evans ten questions about his statements.
Stelle Mr. Evans jetzt zehn Fragen zu seinen Aussagen.
Schreibe die Uhrzeiten aus. Schreibe in Dein Heft.*

Example: 1. When did you get up yesterday morning?
Mr. Evans: I got up at ten to seven.

4. ## A switchboard

*Bilde so viele Fragen wie möglich und gib die Antworten.
Schreibe in Dein Heft.*

Example:
Question: When did you have lunch yesterday?
Answer: I had lunch at twelve o'clock.

Did you	→	get up	
When did you	→	have lunch	yesterday
		watch TV	
Where did you	→	go swimming	last Sunday
		see your friends	
Why didn't you	→	do your homework	
		do the washing up	
		have breakfast	
		play with your friends	
		go to bed	

5. **Fairy tale (Märchen)**

Du kennst sicher das Märchen von "Rotkäppchen" auf deutsch. Auf englisch heißt es "Little Red Riding Hood".
Lies das Märchen sorgfältig durch und unterstreiche alle Verben, die in der Vergangenheit stehen.

Little Red Riding Hood

Once upon a time – so beginnen alle Märchen in englisch – Es war einmal ... (fairy tales).

Once upon a time there <u>was</u> a little girl who <u>lived</u> with her Mum and Dad in the woods. They <u>were</u> all very happy. Every day she put on her pretty little red hood (Kapuze) and went out to play under the trees. The animals in the woods called her "Red Riding Hood". One day little Red Riding Hood's mother came out of the house with a basket on her arm.

"Grandmother is not very well today", she told Little Red Riding Hood. "Walk through the woods and take this basket to her". Little Red Riding Hood took the basket, said goodbye to her mother and went off.

Suddenly she saw a big, hungry old wolf. "Good morning, my dear", said the big bad wolf, "where are you going today?" he asked. "I'm going to see my grandmother", Red Riding Hood answered.

"She is ill and in bed". "Oh, what a pity" said the wolf. "But, let's see who gets there first. I will take one path (Weg) and you take the other". And the big bad wolf ran as fast as he could.

At first the little girl ran, too, but then she saw pretty flowers beside the path and she picked them for her grandmother.

In the meantime (in der Zwischenzeit) the wolf arrived at the grandmother's front door. He knocked at the door. "Who is there?" called the grandmother. "It's Little Red Riding Hood" answered the wolf. "Just open the door and come in", the grandmother called. But when she saw who came in – she jumped out of bed and ran out of the back door.

The big bad wolf put on one of Grandmother's long white night-gowns (Nachthemden), a nightcap and her extra pair of spectacles. Then he jumped into bed.

Knock, knock . . . Little Red Riding Hood opened the door and came in. "Good morning, Grandmother", she said. Then she looked at her grandmother's bed. "Grandmother," she said, "what big eyes you have!" "The better to see you, my dear", answered the big bad wolf.

Then the girl went on, "What big ears you have!". "The better to hear you, my dear", said the big bad wolf. "Oh, but, Grandmother," cried Red Riding Hood, "what big teeth you have!" The wolf jumped out of bed. "The better to eat you, my dear!" he said.

But before the little girl could run the door opened and a woodsman (Holzfäller) ran in with his axe. In a minute the big bad wolf was dead. Then Grandmother came back and they all were very happy.

Exercise 1

Schreibe jetzt die unterstrichenen Verben in Dein Heft und ergänze die restlichen beiden Stammformen, also den Infinitiv und das "past participle". Beispiel: Das erste Verb im Text ist "was".
Du schreibst auf: to be – was/were – been.

Exercise 2

Answer the questions on the text.
Antworte bitte in ganzen Sätzen. Hast Du Schwierigkeiten mit den Fragefürwörtern, sieh auf den Seiten 94 ff. nach.

1. Where did the little girl live with her Mum and Dad?

   The little girl lived with her Mum and Dad in the woods.

2. What did "Red Riding Hood" do every day?

3. What did Mother say to Red Riding Hood one day?

4. What did Red Riding Hood suddenly see in the woods?

5. What did Red Riding Hood do while the wolf was running to Grandmother's house?

6. What did the wolf say after he had knocked at the door?

7. Why did Grandmother jump out of bed and run out of the back door?

8. What did the wolf put on?

9. Who came in?

10. Why did the wolf jump out of bed?

_____

11. Who came in with his axe?

_____

12. What is the German name of the fairy tale "Little Red Riding Hood"?

_____

6. Mixed exercise

Questions in the present tense –
Questions in the past tense

Do/does or did?

*Beginne die folgenden Fragen mit "do/does" oder "did".
Denke dabei an die "signal words", die die entsprechende Zeit anzeigen.*

1. *Did*_____ he buy a car <u>last month</u>?

2. _____ your brother play football <u>every day</u>?

3. _____ your father get up early <u>yesterday</u>?

4. _____ she <u>always</u> go to school by bus?

5. _____ they understand English?

6. _____ you go to school by bus <u>last winter</u>?

7. _____ we play the piano?

8. _____ we play the piano <u>last night</u>?

9. _____ I buy my house <u>in 1970</u>?

10. _____ she meet him <u>long ago</u>?

11. _____ he live in Kiel?

12. _____ you watch TV <u>every</u> evening?

Part 5 Die Verneinung in der Vergangenheit

1. In einem verneinten Satz mit einem Hauptzeitwort mußt Du immer "didn't" (did not) verwenden. Das Zeitwort bleibt in der Grundform.

	Bejahter Satz – Past tense	Verneinter Satz – Past tense
SINGULAR	I, you, he, she, it — opened the window	I, you, he, she, it — didn't open the window
PLURAL	we, you, they — opened the window	we, you, they — didn't open the window
	Verb + -ed (oder unregelmäßig)	didn't + Grundform des Verbs

2. Vervollständige die Satzpaare. (Erinnere Dich an die Formen der unregelmäßigen Verben.)

Bejaht	Verneint

1. He told us all about it. — *He didn't tell us all about it.*

2. _____ — We didn't wait for half an hour.

3. Tom watched television. — _____

4. She began to study English. — _____

5. _____ — Peter didn't ask the teacher.

6. The detective followed the thief. — _____

7. They went to the theatre yesterday. — _____

8. Mother cleaned the rooms last Monday. — _____

Part 6 Past continuous tense

Die Verlaufsform in der Vergangenheit
drückt aus, daß eine Handlung zu einer bestimmten Zeit in der Vergangenheit gerade vor sich ging.

	Person	Form of to **be**	**-ing**-form	
At the moment	I	was	washing	
	you	were	washing	
	he	was	washing	
	she	was	washing	
	it	was	washing	yesterday
	we	were	washing	
	you	were	washing	
	they	were	washing	

Wie Du siehst, wird eine Form von "to be" in der Vergangenheit genommen und **-ing** an die Grundform des Verbs gehängt.

I – he/she/it → was
we – you – they → were
+ **verb** + **-ing**

1. Exercise
Past continuous tense

Die Sätze stehen in der Vergangenheit. Schreibe das Verb im "past continuous tense" daneben.

1. He drove to work in his car.   *was driving*

2. We learnt English.   _____

3. Helen played the violin.   _____

4. They talked about your holidays.   _____

5. She prepared dinner for the whole family. _____

6. You spoke very slowly.   _____

7. I did my homework.   _____

yesterday at 5 o'clock

8. The sky got dark. _____

9. The dog barked at the policeman. _____

10. You helped Mary with the homework. _____

yesterday at 5 o'clock

Part 7   Die Verlaufsform in der Vergangenheit und die einfache Vergangenheit

1. Describing past events

Wenn Du etwas beschreiben willst, was sich in der Vergangenheit gerade abspielte, gebrauchst Du das "past continuous tense".

Dauerte eine Handlung aber bereits eine längere Zeit in der Vergangenheit an, als eine neue Handlung eintrat, so gebraucht man das "simple past" für die neu eintretende Handlung und das "past continuous" für die Handlung, die bereits länger andauerte.

past continuous   simple past
He was writing a letter.   when Mother came in.

das dauerte schon eine Zeit   neue Handlung setzte ein

2. When the lights went out

Dies ist ein Haus, in dem die Leute gestern abend eine Reihe von Tätigkeiten verrichteten.

Plötzlich – um 21.00 Uhr – gab es einen Stromausfall. Schreibe auf, was die Leute in dem Wohnblock taten, als das Licht ausging.
Schreibe in Dein Heft.

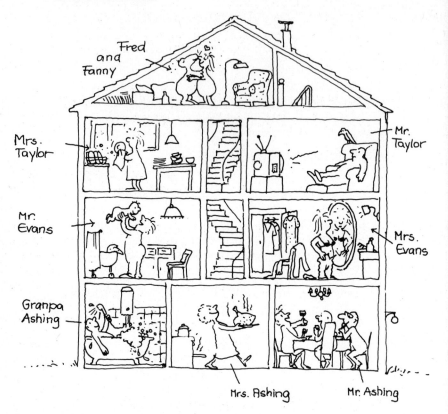

Now say what the people <u>were</u> doing when the lights went out.
These words will help you:

have a bath – wash up – play with his baby – put on her trousers – cook the supper – watch TV – have a dinner.

Example:
1. Mrs. Ashing was cooking the supper when the lights went out.

16 THE PRESENT PERFECT TENSE

Part 1   The forms of the present perfect

Das englische "present perfect" entspricht der deutschen "vollendeten Gegenwart" (Perfekt) nur der Form nach. In der Bedeutung weicht es häufig stark ab.

Während das deutsche Perfekt entweder mit den Hilfsverben "haben" oder "sein" gebildet wird, benützt das englische "present perfect" nur "have/has".

Es besteht aus

> have/has + 3rd form of the verb (past participle)
> **Present Perfect**

Die Formen

			have/has + 3rd form	German	
S I N G U L A R	1st	I	have opened	ich habe geöffnet	Frage: Have you waited? Hast Du gewartet? Verneinung: I have not waited. Ich habe nicht gewartet.
	2nd	you	have waited	du hast gewartet	
	3rd	he she it	has stopped has written has begun	er hat angehalten sie hat geschrieben es hat angefangen	
P L U R A L	1st	we	have asked	wir haben gefragt	
	2nd	you	have lost	ihr habt verloren	
	3rd	they	have arrived	sie sind angekommen	

2.   The 3rd form of the verb (past participle)

Das "past participle" von regelmäßigen Verben wird durch Anhängen von -ed an die Grundform gebildet. Es wird also genau wie das Past von regelmäßigen Verben gebildet und auch so ausgesprochen (siehe S. 146 ff.).

Das "past participle" von unregelmäßigen Verben kannst Du nicht ableiten. Du mußt die Formen lernen (siehe S. 150 ff.). Erst wenn Du diese Formen wie im Schlaf kannst, kannst Du das "present perfect" bilden.

→ | **regular verbs -ed** | **irregular verbs Special Form** |

3. *Hier sind die Formen noch einmal zusammengefaßt. Lies die Sätze in der "vollendeten Gegenwart" laut vor.*

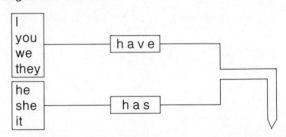

	Grundform	**Past**	**Past participle**
regular verbs	stop	stopped	stopped
	telephone	telephoned	telephoned
	close	closed	closed
	arrive	arrived	arrived
irregular verbs	go	went	gone
	swim	swam	swum
	break	broke	broken
	make	made	made

4. *Fill in the past participle of the verbs.*
Setze die Formen des Mittelwortes der Vergangenheit ein.

1. The thief has _____ the money. (to steal)

2. He's _____ away. (to run)

3. I've just _____ home. (to come)

4. I've _____ breakfast. (to have)

5. Have you ever _____ to London? (to be)

6. Mother has _____ the plates. (to drop)

7. We have already _____ them the pictures. (to show)

8. The wind has _____ the window. (to close)

9. Father has _____ the police. (to telephone)

10. Aunt Lucy has _____ at the station. (to arrive)

11. The teacher has _____ the paper twice. (to fold) (falten)

12. I've _____ the money to my sister. (to give)

13. Have you _____ the pudding yet? (to eat)

Part 2   The present perfect of "to have" and "to be"

Auch die Verben "have" und "be" bilden ihr "present perfect" mit dem Hilfsverb "have/has".

1. Die Formen

to be		to have	
I have been	we have been	I have had	we have had
you have been	you have been	you have had	you have had
he⟩ she has been it⟩	they have been	he⟩ she has had it⟩	they have had

2. Mixed exercise

Setze die Formen des "present perfect" in die Lücken ein.

1. They _**have finished**_ (finish) their breakfast.

2. She (speak) _____ to me about it.

3. We _____ (learn) many new words.

4. They _____ (clean) the house from top to bottom.

5. I _____ (see) that film three times.

6. The boy _____ (be) late for class many times.

7. The girls _____ (play) in the garden.

8. Mr. Evans _____ (teach) many students to speak English.

Part 3   Der Gebrauch der vollendeten Gegenwart

Das "present perfect" wird verwendet, wenn eine Verbindung zwischen Vergangenheit und Gegenwart ausgedrückt werden soll. Denk Dir zwei Kreise:

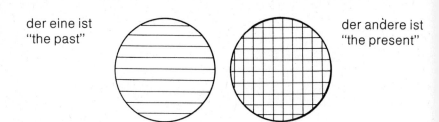

der eine ist "the past"   der andere ist "the present"

Denk Dir nun einen dritten Kreis.
Er ist sowohl Teil der Vergangenheit als auch Teil der Gegenwart.

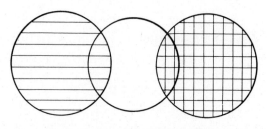

past/present perfect/present

Das "present perfect" steht **erstens,** wenn die Handlung sich unmittelbar vor der Gegenwart ereignet hat und soeben beendet worden ist.

| The plane has just landed. | → Das Flugzeug ist gerade gelandet. Nun ist es da. |
| The teacher has left the classroom. | → Der Lehrer hat gerade das Klassenzimmer verlassen. |

Signalwörter sind hier just (soeben, gerade) – already (schon) – not yet (noch nicht).

3. Ein Hausmann

Mutter ist krank. Vater macht den Haushalt. Schreibe auf, was er gerade tut und was er gemacht hat.

progressive form   **present perfect**

(make)

He is making breakfast.    *He has made breakfast.*

(do the washing-up)

_____   _____

(dry)

_____   _____

(water)

_____   _____

(make)

_____   _____

(wash)

(clean)

(cook)

(lay)

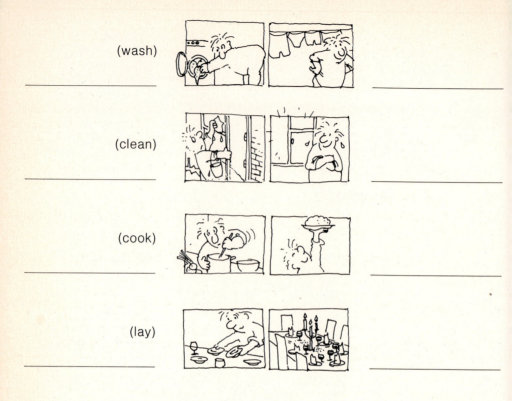

4. Das "present perfect" gibt **zweitens** an, daß ein Vorgang eine deutliche Beziehung zur Gegenwart hat. Im Deutschen läßt sich meist ein "bis heute" ergänzen.

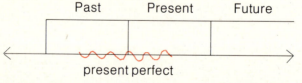

present perfect

Signalwörter sind hier: ever/never (jemals/niemals – im Leben) – up to now, so far (bis jetzt) – not yet (noch nicht).

| Have you ever . . . ? | No, never. | Yes, I . . . |

Stelle die Fragen im "present perfect tense" und beantworte sie für Dich. Schreibe in Dein Heft.

Example: 1. Have you ever smoked cigarettes? No, I haven't.
          2. Have you ever seen a tiger reading a newspaper?

1. smoke cigarettes   2. see tiger read newspaper
3. drive car   4. forget homework   5. lose money
6. fly aeroplane   7. steal apples   8. be in France
9. find purse   10. lose key   11. have budgie (Wellensittich)
12. make cake

5. Das "present perfect" steht **drittens,** wenn ein Vorgang in der Gegenwart noch andauert. Im Deutschen läßt sich ein "jetzt schon" ergänzen.

Signalwörter sind hier **since** (seit) und **for** (schon ... lang, seit)

since bezeichnet einen **Zeitpunkt** (Frage: seit wann?) und steht mit Zeitangaben wie: last year last month August Monday	**for** bezeichnet einen **Zeitraum** (Frage: wie lange schon?) und steht mit Zeitangaben wie: a year a month two weeks three months
Since when have you been in Kiel? I've been in Kiel **since 1978.** Ich bin (schon) seit 1978 in Kiel.	How long have you studied English? I've studied English **for two years.** Ich lerne schon zwei Jahre lang (oder: seit zwei Jahren) English.

Die Wörter "since" und "for" sagen uns, daß der Satz im "present perfect" steht.

Exercise

Welches der untenstehenden Beispiele gibt einen Zeitpunkt (since) oder einen Zeitraum (for) an?
Schreibe die Beispiele geordnet untereinander.

last week – 2 hours – 1970 – Monday – two years – 5 minutes – 1st May – Easter – one o'clock

since	for
last week	

_____ | _____
_____ | _____
_____ | _____
_____ | _____

6.   Setze jetzt jeweils das "present perfect tense" – have/has + past participle – ein.

   1. We are now living in Kiel where we _____ (live) **for** almost seven years.

   2. Mother _____ (be) in hospital **since** July.

   3. Granpa _____ (live) in that house **for** many years.

   4. I _____ (not see) Peter **since** last Christmas.

   5. My car is a Volkswagen. I _____ (have) it **for** three years.

Part 4   "Simple past" and "present perfect"

1.   Im Englischen wird die einfache Vergangenheit, "simple past", benutzt, wenn eine Handlung oder ein Vorgang in der Vergangenheit endgültig abgeschlossen ist.
Signalwörter für die Vergangenheit sind:

2. Das "present perfect" wird benutzt:
1. Wenn ein Vorgang gerade abgeschlossen ist.
2. Wenn ein Vorgang irgendwann in der Vergangenheit begann und bis in die Gegenwart oder darüber hinaus andauert.

Das "present perfect" kann man an folgenden Signalwörtern erkennen:

since	– seit (Zeitpunkt)
for	– seit (Zeitdauer)
ever	– jemals
never	– nie(mals)
not yet	– noch nicht
already	– schon
just	– soeben/gerade

PRESENT PERFECT

3. *Entscheide, in welcher Zeit die Sätze stehen.*
Simple past or present perfect?

	simple past	present perfect
1. I have just seen Brenda.	☐	☒
2. I saw your brother yesterday.	☒	☐
3. I've already done my homework.	☐	☐
4. We've never seen him.	☐	☐
5. Did you watch television last Sunday?	☐	☐
6. She washed her hair on Tuesday.	☐	☐
7. We visited our uncle yesterday.	☐	☐
8. Has the tram come yet?	☐	☐
9. We went to Kiel last week.	☐	☐
10. They have never been to France.	☐	☐
11. I bought it before I went to school.	☐	☐
12. They've arrived!	☐	☐
13. Did we tell them what happened?	☐	☐
14. Have you had breakfast?	☐	☐

4. *Trage jetzt die entsprechenden Zeitformen der Verben ein.*
Überlege jedesmal genau, ob Du das "past tense" oder das "present perfect tense" benutzen mußt.

1. Peter _____ (be) in our class since Christmas.

2. I _____ (see) Brenda a few minutes ago.

3. Father _____ (study) English when he was at school.

4. We are now living in Kiel where we _____ (live) for almost five years.

5. My uncle _____ (be) in America last winter.

6. From 1965–1968 we _____ (live) in Hamburg.

7. We _____ (have) already _____ our breakfast.

8. It _____ just (begin) _____ to rain.

9. My mother _____ (study) French in Paris many years ago.

10. I _____ (see) never _____ a yellow elephant.

5. *Which word must finish the sentence?*
Welches Wort muß den Satz beenden? Kreuze an.

	yet	yesterday
1. They haven't arrived _____.	×	
2. I didn't play with him _____.		×
3. I haven't met him _____.		
4. We haven't seen that film _____.		
5. I didn't go to the cinema _____.		
6. Didn't he telephone you _____.		
7. I haven't had breakfast _____.		
8. They didn't go to Austria _____.		
9. I haven't been to England _____.		
10. She didn't go to school _____.		

6. *Die Zeiten eines Satzes erkennt man auch an den Verbformen. Die folgenden Wörter können nur eine der drei Zeitformen sein.*
Weißt Du welche? Schreibe sie in die richtige Spalte.

Present		**Past**
go		*went*
	fallen ~~broken~~	
	sleep knew hidden	
	draw begun	
	sung took did	
	ridden	
	shown ate	
	ran ~~go~~ ~~went~~	
	hold	
	lose buy lie	

Present perfect *(Setze have/has hinzu.)*

have / has broken

_____

_____

_____

_____

_____

173

17 CONTRACTIONS

Part 1 Die Formen

1. Im Englischen werden häufig in der Umgangssprache verkürzte Formen benutzt.

Regel
Erstens werden das Subjekt eines Satzes und die Formen des Verbs "to be" zusammengezogen

> I'm, you're, he's, she's, it's, we're, they're

Zweitens werden das Subjekt eines Satzes mit den Hilfsverben "will/have" zusammengezogen

> I'll you'll, he'll, she'll, i'll, we'll, they'll
> I've, you've, he's, she's, it's, we've, they've

Drittens werden Hilfsverben und auch alle Formen von "to be" mit dem Wort "not" zusammengezogen

> isn't, wasn't, weren't, won't (= will not), can't, doesn't, don't, didn't, hasn't, haven't

2. **Exercise**
Schreibe die Verkürzungen auf die Linien auf der rechten Seite.

1. We are very busy today.   _we're_

2. He has not spoken to me.   _____

3. It is a very hot day.   _____

4. Father was not able to telephone.   _____

5. They are not going to the theatre with us.   _____

6. They have not many friends in this town.   _____

7. Mr. Scott did not come to the meeting.   _____

8. Mother will not come back until Sunday.   _____

9. He cannot speak English well. _____

10. I do not know her. _____

11. There will be rain tomorrow. _____

12. She is a very nice girl. _____

Index – Stichwortverzeichnis

activities/hobbies 26
asking for help 57
asking the way 76 f.
asking questions 83 ff.,
  92 f., 95, 97 ff., 100 f.
auxiliaries 27
– defective 45 ff.

Bahnhof 107
become 23
be 27 ff., 48 f., 165
Befehlssätze bejaht 66,
  70, 74
– verneint 67
Begrüßung 31
Bitten um Hilfeleistung 57
bring 20
buildings 75

can/cannot/can't 45, 52 f.
classroom phrases 58
contractions 174 f.
continuous form 136 ff.
could/couldn't 45, 52, 55
crossword puzzle 60

do 17 ff., 43 f., 82 f., 119

fairy tale 155 f., 177
false friends 17 ff.
family 42
for 169 f.
Formen des Verbs 9
Fragebildung 83 ff., 92 ff.,
  95, 97
Fragefürwörter 94 f.
Fragestellung in der Vergangenheit 153 f., 158
– mit "be" 48 f.
full verbs 8, 10 ff.
Gegenwartsform 9, 116,
  124 ff., 133 ff., 141 ff.

get 23
getting up 133 f.
getting to school 25

haben = besitzen 41
have 39 f., 165
hear 20 f.
hello 31
Hilfsverben unvollständig
  45 ff.
– vollständig 27
how 96, 104

how many 96
how much 96

imperative 66, 70, 74
ing-form 136
Interrogativ-Pronomen
  94 ff.
interview 100
interviewing people 106

jemanden vorstellen 32
jobs 91, 131 ff.

Körperteile 71 ff.
Kurzformen 174 f.
Kurzfragen 111 ff.

listen to 21
Little Red Riding Hood
  155
let's 70
look 22

make 17 ff.
Märchen 155 f., 177
may 46
must/mustn't 45, 62 ff.

need/needn't 46
negation 89 f., 92 f., 159
negation of "to be" 30

orders 74

parts of the body 71 ff.
past tense 9, 29, 146 ff.,
  170 f.
present tense 9, 28, 116,
  128 f., 133 ff., 141 ff.
present perfect 9, 163 f.,
  166 ff.
progressive form 9, 136,
  139, 141 ff.

question tags 111 ff.
question word 94 ff.
questions 82 ff.

railway station 107 f.
reading comprehension
  23, 65

's' 3. Person Einzahl 116 ff.
Satzstellung 8

Satzstellung bei Hilfsverben 46, 47
see 22
since 169 f.
stare at 22
station 107
street 61 f.
street scene 60 f.

take 20 f.
telling the way 77 ff.
tenses 9, 115
there-structure 35
ticket office 108 f.
traffic 59
traffic lights 60 f.
travelling by train 108

Umschreibung mit do/
  does, did 82 ff., 153 f.,
  157 f.
unregelmäßige Verben
  150 ff.

verabschieden 34
Vergangenheit 9, 28 f., 40,
  146 ff., 161, 170 ff.
vehicles 59, 160
Verkehrszeichen 10 ff.,
  60 f.
Verlaufsform in der
  Gegenwart 9, 136 ff.,
  141 ff.
– in der Vergangenheit 9,
  162
Verneinung in der
  Vergangenheit 159
– mit Hilfsverben 50 ff., 89
– mit "to do" 89 f., 92 f.,
  159
– von "to be" 30
vollendete Gegenwart 9,
  163 f., 166 ff.
– Vergangenheit 10
Vollverben 8, 10 ff.
vorstellen 32

what? 97, 101 f.
when? 98 f., 103, 154
where? 97, 103 f.
which? 96
who? 101 f., 104
why 99, 100, 103
world tour 68 f.
would 56

Zeitstufen 115

176